JUDGING DOLLS

For Collectors, Doll Shows, Investment, Insuring, Appraising, Auction Buying, and Fun

24" doll marked 5-H. Full view on page 114.

by

Mildred Seeley

Photography - Mil Seeley

Cartoons - Duby Seeley

Cover, this 10X Jumeau (see page 7 full view) was so good the judges could not find any reason to deduct points.

MILDRED SEELEY'S EDJS EDUCATIONAL DOLL JUDGING SYSTEM

Mildred Seeley's Educational Doll Judging System

Introducing a plan for judging dolls that will increase the number of exhibitors, as well as encourage and educate the dollmaker and doll collector. At the same time, this system will stimulate the public's awareness of dolls through education.

Dedication

To Vernon, my wonderful husband, who works with me on all my doll projects.

NOTICE: The information in this book is true and complete to the best of our knowledge. All recommendations are made without guarantees on the part of the authors or the publishers. The authors and publishers disclaim all liability in connection with the use of the information. All dolls are from the author's collection unless otherwise noted.

Left, Rare Jumeau Character 208, 26". "So they awarded you blue ribbons, rosettes, evertything—who wouldn't howl with happiness?"

Scott PUBLICATIONS
SCOTT PUBLICATIONS
30595 8 MILE
LIVONIA, MI 48152-1798

Library of Congress #90-063280
PRINTED IN USA

1ST
REGION 8

Introduction

We have long needed a book on judging or evaluating dolls. This book can only touch on all the important information that is needed. It can only set the collectors' and dollmakers' minds in the right direction. My aim is to start everyone thinking. Thinking always precedes action.

This book is for *all* doll people. It is for the collector, the dollmaker, the studio operator, and the doll dealer. All and every doll lover will use this book to judge dolls every day. It may serve to make the reader more aware and provide a tool in the actual judging of dolls. It will also serve as the ultimate in preparing dolls for competition.

Judging Dolls does not promise to train judges from scratch, nor can it cover every aspect of judging dolls. Everyone realizes that there are thousands of dolls with no two dolls exactly alike.

A person cannot decide to be a doll judge today and judge tomorrow. It takes not one book but many, along with dedication to prepare and study. A lifetime of doll collecting and dollmaking makes the best basic training.

All of us, dollmakers and doll collectors, judge dolls every day. We do not think of it as judging dolls, but that is what we are doing. We go to a dollmaking class, and we unconsciously judge the instructor's dolls. Or, we judge the doll the student next to us is making. We also stand back and judge our own "masterpieces."

For example, a collector may go to a doll show wanting to buy a doll. Before the day is over, she may have judged fifteen dolls before settling on one to buy.

Or, the collector or dollmaker visits a friend's doll collection, and he or she judges the dolls in view. I know both the collector and the visiting friend would be horrified at the idea of either of them "judging" each other's dolls, but this is what happens without the awareness of either party. People who love dolls cannot look at them without, in some way, either consciously or subconsciously, evaluating them.

In the chapters ahead we are going to judge dolls for our own collections. We will see how museums select dolls. We will see how to do doll appraisals. Most of all, we will find out how dolls are judged at shows and realize that most of the rules apply to any kind of doll judging.

Think of judging as an educational exercise to make you a better collector—to make your collection a better collection. Think of all doll judging as a fun thing that must not be taken so seriously that it takes the joy out of dollmaking or doll collecting.

Left, 27" Steiner Figure A No. 6. Excellent bisque, all hand-sewn antique dress. Steiner shoes.

I have used the word *she* for a collector, dollmaker and judge—this is a matter of convenience. Men and women collect, make and judge dolls. Often, men's collections are superior, and dolls made by men equal those made by women. Each year the *Millie Award* is given to the best dollmaker. In 1983, a man won the award.

I have also used the words *artist, reproduction, original, antique, collectible, and modern* to describe dolls. There are several types of dolls and just as many definitions to go along with them. For the purposes of clarity and consistency, the following definitions apply to these types of dolls. An *artist* doll is one made by a doll artist from his or her own original idea and sculpture. A *reproduction* doll is a reproduction of either an antique or modern doll for commercial or other purposes. An *original* doll is a one-of-a-kind doll. An *antique* doll must be over 75 years old; a *collectible* doll must be 75 to 35 years old; and a *modern* doll is 0 to 35 years old.

This book is filled with examples of blue ribbon dolls. These dolls are mostly French because my collection is made up mostly of French dolls. All blue ribbon dolls are important whether they are paper dolls, tiny all-bisque dolls, or the expensive German characters.

We sometimes think of "mint" and "unplayed with" condition as being synonymous with blue ribbon, but with dolls we need to add "quality" to both definitions. With reproduction dolls, blue ribbon means "superb craftsmanship" and "enduring beauty."

To all people everywhere, blue ribbon means winner. To all doll people, blue ribbon means an outstanding doll. We think of blue ribbon as a reward to the person who owns the doll or has made the doll. It is something like receiving a degree, a great honor. In France, the term *cordon bleu* was used to distinguish noblemen who became members of a special order. They wore a blue ribbon. This probably is where the idea of the blue ribbon started.

Right, 23" uncataloged Jumeau Character 10X. This is a super doll in super condition, all original, unplayed with.

Table of Contents

PART II

Getting the Judging Message Known

Each time there is a call for dolls for a convention or doll show, or a competitors' exhibit, a short explanation should be printed similar to the paragraphs below. This should be printed over and over until it becomes known to all the doll clubs and their members. It should be brought to the attention of members at club meetings, posted in doll studios, and printed in publications until it completely changes would-be-exhibitors' attitudes to: "I am an exhibitor."

Explanation of Seeley Educational Doll Judging System

Each doll is to be judged individually on its own merits. If a doll is excellent, it deserves a blue ribbon regardless of how many excellent dolls there are. If a doll is good, it will receive a red ribbon; fair, a white ribbon. If the doll is poor, no ribbon will be awarded even if it is the only doll in its class.

Remember, the Seeley Educational Doll System is meant to encourage dollmaking and educate the dollmakers as to where and how they can improve their dollmaking.

Each and every doll exhibited in the correct category will receive an "exhibit ribbon." This will show the doll was exhibited in such-and-such a year in whatever category. (There will be times when small clubs will feel they cannot afford to do this.)

Dolls will compete against each other for Best of Class and Best of Show.

Right, in practice session the judges gave this Kestner 180 a blue ribbon, because his bisque is good and he is in excellent condition. He is considered rare and appealing. His blue serge suit is either antique or made of old material.

Collectible and Antique Doll Exhibits

There are several reasons for collectible and antique doll exhibits. The first is obvious—to make the convention or show *better attended* because there is *something special to see and without additional cost*. Many people, like myself, will attend a convention or show mainly to see and study closely the finest dolls the collectors own, and to get to see and know rare dolls.

Exhibiting dolls is great for increasing attendance at doll shows or conventions. *Education* is the main reason for exhibiting collectible and antique dolls. When the public sees what is being collected in the way of old dolls, their interest cannot remain dormant.

I've listened to people going to a doll exhibit for the first time. They see a doll and exclaim, "That one is like the one I had when I was seven." Or, "I know where there is a doll like that one, only in better condition." And, "Maybe my old doll is still in mother's attic." Before the end of the exhibit a new doll collector has been inspired or perhaps several prospective new collectors have their interest awakened. This is one of the reasons for exhibiting dolls, to inspire new collectors.

Or, the novice doll collector goes to an exhibit and views the many dolls in the exhibit with quite a different idea. She spends much of her time studying the baby dolls and the German character dolls. Up until this time, she has collected baby dolls and a few open mouth dolls—all German. She passes up the French dolls, because she feels they are too expensive to even think about. With only a few years of collecting under her belt, she studies the dolls and tries to figure out why certain baby dolls have blue ribbons. It isn't difficult to see that the blue ribbon dolls are older, in better condition, and to her surprise, wear original clothing. Now, she immediately realizes a mistake she has been making. She has removed the old clothes and made spanking new dresses for her old baby dolls. From the exhibit, the new collector has learned a very valuable lesson which will aid her future collecting.

Now she studies the German character dolls. She never realized how many different and interesting faces there are. In fact, she has never seen a German character doll except in a book. It is different meeting the dolls face-to-face. The collector makes a decision and tells herself, "Instead of the next three dolly faced dolls that I might buy in a year, I am going to save and buy a K*R and/or an Armand Marseille character with a closed mouth."

Another scenario might be an experienced collector who hasn't added a doll to her collection in three or four years. She has many fashion dolls, so she wishes to compare the fashion dolls on exhibit to hers. She is awed to find two blue ribbon fashion dolls that she has never seen in a book and on bodies she never knew existed. Her collecting fire is quickly rekindled and after studying the dolls, she knows she has to buy these dolls or similar ones for her collection. The exhibit has fired up the would-be stagnant collector to new heights of enthusiasm. The collector goes home and instantly stirs up the enthusiasm of her whole club.

Right, Country Fair Kids, Max and Moritz. They are rare enough to be almost certain of a blue ribbon.

ALDERNEY DAIRY CO.
BRIDGE STREET
NEWARK, N.J

The middle-of-the-road and advanced collectors go to the exhibits to see and learn. Every exhibit that I have attended has had some rarely seen dolls. There is always something worth seeing and chronicling in your notes.

The doll costumer will find numerous dolls with original outfits. She will immediately know how that type of doll was originally dressed. Even better than glancing at an original costume is the opportunity to study the costume up close. There is nothing that says she cannot take notes and make sketches. She can usually tell the fabric and even see how the fine details were executed.

The doll exhibit is a costumer's ultimate authority in how and what the doll should wear.

An exhibit of antique dolls is just what dollmakers need to see. Many dollmakers have worked for years from photographs of old dolls. They use photos to get the eyebrows, lips and lashes correct. The ultimate is seeing the old doll from which a reproduction is being made. Seeing the actual colors and how the doll is wigged and dressed is an opportunity for the dollmaker to check her work and expand her knowledge of the old doll.

Doll exhibits are an excellent opportunity for doll study clubs to get ideas to bring back to their members. They can even bring back photos or slides for the group to study. All dolls are in classes and many times there is an expert (usually a judge) who can give even more information on the dolls exhibited.

There is no way to thank the wonderful doll collectors, who chance the wear and tear of their precious dolls and take the effort and the time to exhibit. Even if every person who saw the doll writes a thank you note, there really is no way to show appreciation for these collectors' efforts. Their only reward comes from knowing that they have shared or contributed to the total success of a show or convention.

Perhaps a collector's doll gets a ribbon and this can give her a good feeling as well as add more esteem to the doll. But even a Best of Class will hardly make up for the effort it takes to get the doll registered and into the exhibit. I wonder who thanks those whose dolls receive no award, no ribbon, and yet make judging possible for the other dolls, and increase the number of dolls for the attending public to view.

There is always a little promotion by dealers with the exhibiting of antique and collectible dolls. A blue ribbon on a doll will increase its chances of selling, giving the dealer an opportunity to showcase her dolls while increasing the public's awareness about what she has for sale. Exhibiting dolls is good business.

Above, dealers exhibit their dolls with their ribbons, because dolls with ribbons bring higher prices.

V'Lou Oliveira, OK

Reproduction Doll Exhibits

The doll show or convention would not be complete without a full exhibit of all the different types of dolls reproduced. Exhibiting increases the general public's awareness about what is being made, and it encourages people who have never tried dollmaking to get started and make a doll.

The reproduction doll exhibit, which showcases many different areas and instructors, offers the dollmakers an opportunity to compare their work with the best from other dollmakers.

The exhibit gives exposure to many molds from many mold companies. Then, the dollmaker sees finished dolls from these molds and this, in turn, promotes sales.

A fine exhibit of dolls always helps the company whose dolls have been used. It also promotes doll sales for those producing the beautiful, authentic reproduction dolls. Exhibits of good dolls promote the doll studios where the dolls were made, and the products used on these dolls increases the sales for doll stores or studios.

From the dollmaker's point-of-view, why does the dollmaker exhibit her dolls? Many doll artists have a built-in urge to compete. They need to feel that their doll is tops, the very best.

But really, the dollmaker's main goal in exhibiting is to get a critique of her doll efforts. She needs to know just how her work compares.

Louise Mathisen, CA

Edna Miller, TX

Julie Stringer, IL

Photos of reproduction dolls that were trophy winners, Millie winners, and blue ribbon winners.

Emma Lou Keike

Karen Smith, MO

Robin Taylor, NV

Karen Milk, NV

Josie Mull, LA

Kathy Zoch, IL

Diane Arneson, IL

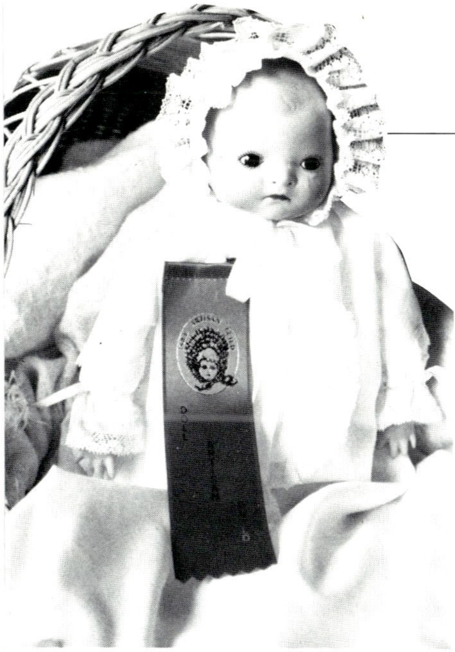

Worldwide dollmaking talents are shown in these prize-winning dolls.

Vicki Inouye, Canada

Remona Gibeson, MO

Ruth Royce, CO

Jean Mantz, WA

Pam Jackson, New Zealand

Lois Nuth, Canada

Earning a blue ribbon gives a sense of top achievement and with it comes fun, joy and the good feeling of having "made it." There is nothing more exhilarating, more exciting, or more encouraging than earning a blue ribbon.

The judging of a doll, using my method, is always meant to *encourage* the dollmakers to make more dolls *and* to make better dolls. If judging is done correctly and dollmakers understand the judging, the dollmaker should come away encouraged and helped even if she doesn't win an award.

The following list is the purpose of this judging system for reproduction and artists dolls:

1. To promote and encourage the making of reproduction and artists dolls.
2. To raise the standard of quality to the highest level by:
   a. encouraging all dollmakers to improve their work by awarding ribbons, prizes and praise.
   b. giving constructive criticism without discouraging the dollmaker.
3. To make uniform and fair rules for all judging of reproduction and original dolls worldwide.
4. To promote the use of trained and certified judges.
5. To encourage exhibits at all doll shows.
6. To standardize the procedures for becoming a certified judge.
7. To have enough certified judges to cover even the smallest shows.
8. To standardize ribbon colors.
9. To standardize judging point systems and score sheets.
10. To standardize the use of exhibit cards with each doll in order to:
    a. aid and improve the judging.
    b. improve the educational value to the public.
11. To educate to judge against the *antique* doll and not against the other dolls in the competition.
12. To develop a good educational philosophy and attitude in all judges.

Right, 30" number 13 Long Face Jumeau in antique dress and bonnet. These are always a good bet for a blue ribbon.

Judges Training

Suggested Requirements for Judges

1. Take a two-day intensive study course with an expert or judge in the Seeley Educational Doll Judging System to:
   a. understand and practice the Seeley Educational Doll Judging System.
   b. study the judging and exhibiting systems theory.
   c. understand the educational value of exhibit cards on dolls.
   d. learn to encourage and stimulate collectors and doll-makers through judging.
2. Have firsthand experience in the study of antique dolls. Visit museums and attend auction seminars and auction previews to examine costumes and painting.
3. Have a simulated, hands-on judging experience with instruction.
4. Know how to use reference materials and have your own collection of reference books (successful judging is based on adequate information).
5. Upon completing the study course, practical experience as a working judge is necessary. Volunteer your services as an assistant or a recorder for a judge. You must work with at least two different judges, after which, you will be certified.
6. It is further suggested that you work with a seasoned judge for your first assignment.
7. Make at least a few dolls.

Note: Requirements 5 and 6 do not apply to those who are already judges and changing over to the Seeley Educational Doll Judging System.

Preparing to be a Judge

A successful judge needs years of experience judging dolls. There are plenty of good experiences that will help a judge prepare for the major task of judging a doll show. She can volunteer to judge doll class work, or small exhibits held in studios, or even the evaluation of a single doll. She should attend every doll show possible and practice judging the dolls exhibited. Museums are a good place to study the painting and costumes on the antique doll. Auction previews are another possibility for training. Aspiring judges must gain practice wherever they can.

Another source of aid for the judge is books with doll photographs as well as doll auction catalogs. With these the judge marks her memory with the many doll faces that she will either see reproduced, or on the antique dolls exhibited.

Of course, a lifetime of doll study and dollmaking makes the best background for a judge, but a good memory and an intensive study of old dolls can do a lot. Clubs can help by having a simulated competition so members will know how dolls are judged, while at the same time giving potential judges experience. (See letter from Susan Foreman pg. 103).

Aside from training, a good judge should have good eyesight; physical stamina during the sometimes long hours of judging; and enough character to stand behind her decision when faced with a complaining exhibitor. Integrity must be at the basis of judging, because it takes courage to stand by impartial decisions. It is most important that the judge be fair-minded and have a sincere desire to promote dolls. She must judge just the doll, *not* the dollmaker or collector. She must not be partial or hold a grudge. She must have tireless patience while judging the poor dolls because these will gain the most from the judging. She must be thorough, and she must follow the rules. Tact and kindness are the essence during the "judge-meet-exhibitor." Criticism must be gentle and constructive to have any value. This kind of treatment will encourage the exhibitor to try again.

In preparing to judge, collect good, quick reference books to take with you. If you are judging reproduction dolls or antique dolls, be sure you are comparing the face to an *antique* doll. Many catalogs have photos of reproductions and some technique sheets have photos of dolls done by doll artists. Study your books all the time, and be up-to-date on the research available.

Some shows will collect a stack of reference books for the judges to use, but usually a judge must carry her own books. Judging is faster when using familiar reference books. Some judges will wish to specialize in certain types of dolls because this is what the person collects or makes. It depends on the length of time and amount of study that has gone into that particular field.

If the judge is an experienced dollmaker, she will have the proper background to effectively criticize the reproduction doll, and to explain to the exhibitor exactly why, for example, the brushstrokes or the doll's finish are not perfect. The maker of reproduction dolls will have a more thorough knowledge of what molds are on the market and will be able to recognize those dolls from the molds at a glance. The dollmaker will also know about bisque; the formation of the facial features; kiln cracks; warping; and the setting of eyes. She still may have to use her reference materials to check for correctness of lashes, brows or lips. Being a dollmaker gives her firsthand experience with the difficulties in the dollmaking process. Then, she can explain to the exhibitor how to improve her doll, or tell her how great her doll really is.

The judge of any kind of doll must always have in mind the necessity of encouragement. Never say anything that will in any way discourage dollmaking or collecting. The whole idea behind judging is to encourage doll collecting and making. We want to show examples that will inspire and encourage others to join in the fun of dolls.

A course in judging helps make better judges. Here's one that was held in my home.

And practice helps, too.

The antique doll judge must be endowed with all these same characteristics plus an ever-expanding knowledge of all the different doll categories. Again, the study of antique dolls, wherever possible, is the main tool along with a good memory. And a longtime collector with an intimate knowledge of all kinds of dolls has an advantage, too.

Never get the idea that even after you have been trained and completed extensive study in new or old dolls that you are going to know everything or operate without mistakes. We must keep in mind that we are not perfect and few of our undertakings will be exactly perfect. Be prepared for some misgivings on your part and some complaints from "perfect people."

Doll judging will come easier after you have developed a method of judging and worked at it for a period of time. Remember, judging is not something you can learn overnight. Later, after you have realized how many people you have helped to be better, more confident dollmakers, you will reap the joys from the hard work of judging.

When I go to conventions, sometimes people I don't know will throw their arms around me and tell me that I made them blue ribbon winners with a little constructive criticism. That makes me feel great.

Once a judge is trained and certified and gained some experience, then any club should be able to hire the judge knowing she is properly trained and can do the job efficiently without too many problems.

Judges are important people.

Pay for Judges

Most doll shows are run with volunteer help, and at first thought it may seem strange that the judges should be paid. But upon closer examination this is not true. For example, the judge must have some background and interest in the dolls she is judging. Also, certified judges must complete specialized study which costs them their time, transportation and the expense of the course. She may even have to purchase several reference books to supplement her knowledge and extend her skills. The judge puts in long, hard hours trying to be as exacting and as diplomatic as possible —standing behind her decisions and meeting exhibitors face-to-face.

Judges must also make certain that everyone goes home happy with her praise, ribbons and constructive criticism. The judge for the show, or the judging team is not replaceable in any way; they are the most important part of the exhibit room. It is the judges who make the exhibit room a success or a disaster. This all boils down to making the doll show a calamity or an ongoing wonderful occasion for all concerned. Each year that there is bad judging it damages the show for the following year(s).

Many judges are paid by giving them a table(s) or a booth at the show. Some clubs work out an exchange of judges. And some clubs pay for their judges' training and expect them to judge a couple of shows in return.

All kinds of arrangements and exchanges can be worked out that are satisfactory to the show and to the judges.

Probably the best way is to pay the judge and pay her well!

Judges Workload

In a very large show you might have 250-350 dolls to be judged. This is a lot of dolls to be carefully gone over and judged. Eight judges can do this satisfactorily in two days. Judges usually work in pairs, making four pairs of judges. Each team will judge 60 plus dolls. Judging sheets will be made out and criticism written.

Some judges will have fifty dolls, some only two or three. The doll classes are never evenly divided. Some dolls take a lot more time to judge than others, so judges are asked to help judge other classes so everyone finishes at about the same time.

Sometimes it works out well to give a seasoned judge a beginner to work with. The beginner may or may not be paid her first time. This is a good way for beginners to get the necessary training and for shows to save money.

It is always difficult to know just how many dolls the show will have and how many judges are needed, unless all the dolls are preregistered.

No two judging situations are exactly the same, because there are thousands of different antiques and molds from which reproductions are produced. Also, categories set up for shows differ yearly, because every category cannot be covered each year.

With the exhibit cards, trained judges, and judging sheets that explain where *and* the maximum points that can be taken off, the judging will be fair and accurate. The judges will have to make some minor decisions on the spot, but this is why we have trained judges.

The yet unjudged French reproductions. Competition is keen because each artist has done her very best.

Judges Follow-up

If at all possible, there should be a short meeting of the judges and the show committee directly following the judging. This often takes the form of a judges luncheon, tea or dinner get-together. It must be held where the judges and the committee can talk without being overheard.

Here the committee and judges will have a frank discussion of the set-up, the categories and the number of dolls judged. All complaints and suggestions from the judges are voiced so that improvements are implemented before the next show. The judges can also explain what common faults were found with the dolls, and these can be corrected by getting the message back to the teachers, studios and collectors.

Actual Judging

The judge must develop a system so that all entries get the same treatment. The last doll of the day should have the same attention and time as the very first dolls.

Judges can develop their own system, or they can use the one I have used and taught for years. First, *reread* what the entrance sheet says concerning the rules for that category.

Suppose there are twenty French reproduction dolls in the "Milette" class. These small dolls are all about the same size. First, I line them up. Then, I go down through the line checking general appearance and reading exhibit cards. I move to the front all the dolls that generally look like blue ribbon winners. I push to the back any dolls that give the impression they may be fair or not ribbon winners. Now I have three lines of dolls. These lines will change as I go carefully over each doll. In the "Milette" class there will be Jumeaux, Brus, Schmitts and other French dolls all exhibited together. I must know how the antique doll from each of these companies was painted, and a handy reference book like *Project-Milettes* will give me a quick reference to the old doll. If I know a day or so in advance that I will be judging that particular group of dolls, I will get out the book and study the painting. This will speed up my judging and improve my accuracy. Never think that everyone will remember everything in a category even though it is their special field.

This same technique of using reference books and study can be applied to any group of dolls.

Always keep in mind with this judging system that we are judging against an ideal, not the other dolls in that class.

While studying the dolls in order to judge painting, smoothness of bisque, clothing, etc., the doll may be carefully picked up, looked under, and even the bonnet or shoes removed if necessary.

Now carefully study each doll individually and mark its score on the sheet. After judging all the sections, first add good comments, then constructive criticism.

As you're working, you will probably push some dolls to the second row or perhaps even to the third row.

Work over the second row. If you find one that should have been in the first row, move it up for a blue ribbon. Check the workmanship of the rest of the dolls down the line. Be sure to add good comments, as well as remarking on what needs improvement.

The hardest to judge are the dolls in the "fair" group or white ribbon winners, as well as those that will receive no ribbons. These must be given more time. You must figure out where these dollmakers need to improve and tell them. Tell them not only what needs improving, but how it can be done. Plan, too, on seeing these dollmakers at the end of the show.

If there is any question in the judge's mind about which ribbon to award, always give the exhibitor the benefit of the doubt and give the next highest ribbon. Happiness is an exhibitor! Even if it is a borderline case, it is apt to bring the exhibitor back another year and with an improved doll.

Above, Marion Mowle, Canada

Judges should work out a system of judging so that the last doll gets as much attention as the first.

I cannot put too much emphasis on the comments written on the judging sheet. This part of judging impresses the exhibitor most. A judge's suggestions can work to improve the quality of dolls for the next show, and they help people to feel good about their exhibits.

Try in every way not to hurt the exhibitor's feelings with your attitude or comments. Realize this is an educational type of judging, and *educating* is the sole purpose of the judging.

Finish marking the sheets and pinning on the ribbons. If you have second thoughts, mark them higher. Be generous.

This "row movement" method is only one of several methods for preparing to judge dolls. A judge can develop her own system, making sure her system provides equal treatment for all the dolls.

Pan doll reproduction by Barbara Ota.

The Point System

I must again emphasize the importance of judges training. Judges need training in this system, with exhibit cards, and the score sheets in this book. They need practice and experience in order to know how many points to deduct for this or that. This system allows the judge to judge one section of the doll at a time.

Ordinarily, I like to work in the positive manner. But after working with lots of judges over the years, I found it easier and quicker to deduct points, because the numbers are smaller. Both experienced and inexperienced judges find it easier to add up the smaller numbers and deduct the total from 100 to get the final score. A quick glance tells if a math error has been made. Believe me—judges are not all great mathematicians. Use pencil when scoring, it makes it easier to change mistakes.

Reproduction Dolls

What to Expect From the Reproduction Doll

The reproduction doll should look like the antique doll did on Christmas morning about one hundred years ago. She should be crisp and perfect.

The painting and coloring of the face should be an exact and faithful copy (misplaced accent lines, etc. are considered errors and are not copied). The wig must be made of either mohair or human hair. And whether it was made or purchased, it must be styled and groomed. Her costume is fresh with new materials that are pressed and perfect. The materials are only natural—silks, cottons, linens or wool—as was used when *the antique* was made. The underclothing consists of the same garments as the antique doll would have worn, such as chemise, drawers, one or two petticoats, and perhaps a corset. All underclothing was made from white cotton or linen with the exception of the often found flannel petticoat. The petticoats and drawers were held up by drawstrings or gathered on a band and buttoned. The older dolls wore split drawers. Some chemises were long, others came just below the hips. Some had buttons and buttonholes on the shoulder, and some just had big neck holes.

Patty Chaddock, IL

Lee Bryant, CO

Cathy Storey,
S. Australia

A talented group, these dollmakers.

Look at all the prize winners.

Douglas Coats, CA

Left,
Suzanne Pirtle,
Tucson, AZ

Right,
Sherry Williams,
NY

The dress length on the children dolls was just to the bottom of the ball in the knee joint.

The children dolls wore socks. Some wore hats or bonnets and some did not. Made or commercial shoes are accepted.

On old dolls, both machine and hand stitching were used. It is generally accepted for appearance's sake that hems and places that show should be hand sewn.

Antique clothing, shoes or wigs are *not* accepted.

Dolls with pierced ears should have earrings. Brus, A.T.'s and Jumeaux came with beads around the joint in the neck.

The body will be composition if the antique doll had a composition body, leather if the antique was leather. Bisque is accepted only in tiny dolls when the original body was bisque. The body should be in correct proportion, and it is best to have a French body on a French doll, a German body on a German doll.

Alice Lester's doll is a fine example of where "bonus points" would be great. Her mother, Alice Levrett carved and finished this copy of a Phenix body.

Bonus Points

An Australian judging sheet for reproduction dolls has "Bonus Points." In several of my classes we discussed this idea. Most agreed that it was a good idea.

Bonus points could be given for such things as sleep eyes that work, wobbly tongues, handmade shoes and wigs, and hand-sewn dresses, or something else that was very special.

This would be a way of calling attention to special talents or special efforts. It could in some instances break a tie for the Best of Class Rosette. Although awarding bonus points would make more work for the judges, these points would encourage dollmakers to "go that extra mile" with each doll they exhibited.

These would be added on to the judging sheets at the bottom as "+ 1 for wig."

Judging Costumes on Artists and Reproduction Dolls

Dolls entered in dollmaking competitions are always costumed. The dolls would not make an attractive display if they were not costumed. Actually, the costume is a part of the whole and should be judged with the doll. It is the costume that complements or completes the character.

Many or most dollmakers are fine craftsmen with original ideas, but being a fine seamstress is not always one of their skills. To compensate, many dollmakers will plan and design the costume and even purchase the appropriate material. Then, they have a seamstress do the actual sewing. There are other dollmakers who feel they should, and do, complete the whole doll—sewing included.

All this costume business makes judging difficult. For example, a fine seamstress on the judging team may want to count off for every poor stitch in the costume.

V'Lou Oliveira shows her costuming talents.

Reproduction dolls placed in competition should be dressed. These dolls were made and dressed by the apprentice judges.

Before judging begins, the judges should be informed about how they will be judging the costumes. Better yet, contestants should be informed when the contest is originally planned about costume judging.

The dolls cannot be judged without their costumes, because the costume is a part of the doll. And to judge the costumes as though it were a contest for *seamstresses*, instead of *dollmakers*, would not be fair. So we must come to a conclusion about judging costumes before the dolls are put in competition.

There should be a separate class for doll costumers where the *doll* is not judged, except in relation to the appropriateness of the costume for the doll wearing it.

We have come to the conclusion that reproduction dolls in competition can be dressed by anyone the dollmaker chooses. Unless, of course, there is a separate class for dolls made completely by the dollmaker, including bodies, clothing, wigs, shoes, et al.

Pamela Jackson's Googly is dressed exactly as she should be.

Points to consider while judging:

1. Decide if the dress fits correctly (the appropriate size and length for the doll).
2. Notice that appropriate material was used for the doll; it cannot be too thick, large or heavy.
3. Note if it complements the doll's face, calling attention to her face and not overwhelming the doll.
4. Judge the quality of the stitching only if it takes away from the overall appearance of the doll (the hemming should be invisible or done by hand).
5. Note the completeness of the costume, including a bonnet, drawers, petticoat, chemise, or whatever the old doll would have worn.

The complete costume should be judged from a distance to visualize the doll as a whole. Notice if it "carries out" the dollmaker's original idea, and if it enhances and calls attention to the doll's face.

There should be no controversy over the judging of dolls' costumes. Think of the costume as a contributing factor that the dollmaker has chosen to enhance her doll. Think of the costume as you would think of the wig—something the dollmaker has selected to bring out the beauty of the doll.

Suggestions for Reproduction Doll Judges

- When there is something that puzzles you about a reproduction doll exhibit, consult with another judge or the exhibit chairman.
- If there is something you are not sure about, do not hesitate to ask another judge.
- If there is a doll you have never seen, and you are unsure of the painting; check with a book, catalog or another judge. Don't guess.
- Don't waste time judging dolls that have been entered into the wrong category or class.
- Be sure that none of your students' dolls are entered in the groups you are judging.
- Examine and study every doll.
- Give the last doll or doll group just as much care and time as you did the first dolls.
- Be careful not to let your personal likes or dislikes enter into your decision.
- Remember how important your job is to the exhibitor and how she will feel when she reads your comments.
- Always make some positive comments before telling an exhibitor how she can improve and where.
- Never shrink from meeting the exhibitor. If you have done your job conscientiously, and you are trained to judge; you know what you are doing.
- On the whole, the comments on the evaluation sheet should tell the exhibitor all she needs to know about where she can improve.
- People not receiving a ribbon should have a consultation with an expert or one of the judges, so they will be aware of problem areas. They should go home happy with the desire to improve next time.
- Do not let a beautiful bonnet sway you on a poor doll.
- Be sure you are judging the doll, not the dollmaker.
- Be very careful in judging black dolls, because their painting mistakes do not show easily.

A close-up of Jamie Englert's painting.

Judging the First Reproduction Doll

Let me take you by the hand and lead you through the judging of one reproduction doll. This way you will look through my eyes and see what I see. We will record our decisions on the judging sheet and come up with the proper ribbon.

This can be a pattern for judging reproduction dolls in general. This doll is entered in the French Reproduction Children class, 15" to 24".

Stand back and we will judge the overall appearance of the doll. Does she look like the antique? Yes. We think she looks very much like the old doll. Her costume is a copy of the old doll's—not just the dress, but the bonnet, and wig. Her proportion is perfect. We took off no points under overall appearance.

Now we must study the painting. Here we will move in and study the doll at very close range. First we check the blushing on the cheeks, is it well-blended? The blushing is perfect, it flows into the flesh color without any abrupt stopping points. It is darker where it should be darker.

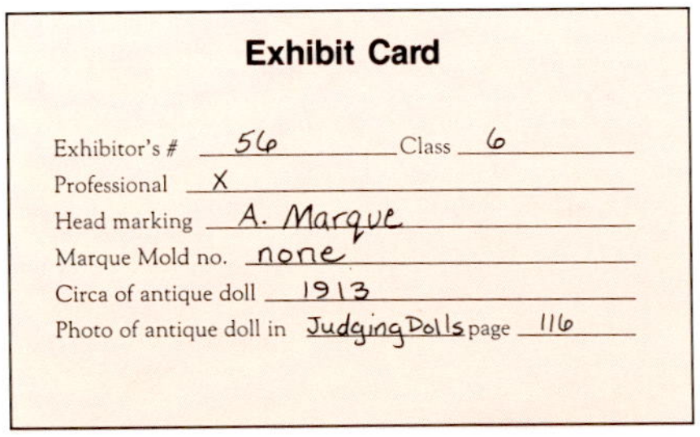
Exhibit Card

Exhibitor's # 56 Class 6
Professional X
Head marking A. Marque
Marque Mold no. none
Circa of antique doll 1913
Photo of antique doll in Judging Dolls page 116

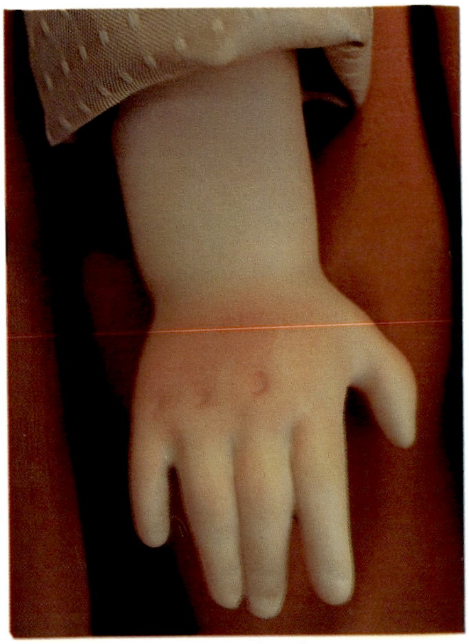
Reproduction Marque hands.

This reproduction is a Marque.

Lashes and brows are painted a little differently on Marques.

These shoes are not like an antique Marque's shoes.

Check out the doll's brows. Are the shape and placement correct? Is the color right? The same must be judged on the lashes—the color, shape, the artist's skill of application. On the lips, study the way the color is applied and is it the right color?

The eyebrows, lashes, and mouth on this doll look very much like the old doll. The overall coloring and blending is nearly perfect. We will take off no points in the painting section.

Now comes the finishing or workmanship of the doll. Study her bisque hands. See if the neck fits the body hole. Check the body using white cotton gloves. Check the eye cut and fitting. Be sure the eye cutting is not too large or too small. Be sure the eye holes are beveled and that the glass eyes are similar to the model.

The finishing on this doll is very professionally done. Everything fits on the body. The eyes are properly cut and beveled. The choice of eyes is good. I can't find a place where a point should be deducted, can you?

We will look at the costume from a distance and again up close. We will carefully lift her dress, check underclothing, then shoes and socks.

The doll's dress and bonnet are a faithful copy of the antique Marque. The quality of the material is excellent, the fit and sewing excellent. Actually we could find no place to take off points until we came to the shoes. The shoes look large and clumsy for this fine doll. They could have been more like the antique Marque's. We will take off two points.

This is a very fine reproduction doll. She was easier to judge than a very poor doll. This excellent doll will set a standard for you. You know how an "excellent" doll should be done.

MILDRED SEELEY'S EDJS EDUCATIONAL DOLL JUDGING SYSTEM

Reproduction Dolls

To customize this form, place the name of your show here... ...then photocopy.

		POINTS DEDUCTED
I. Overall appearance	**30 Points**	
Similarity to antique doll	1-15	
Costume, wig and shoes appropriate for doll	1-5	
Proportion of head to body	1-10	
	TOTAL	0
II. Painting	**35 Points**	
Cheek and other blending, smoothness and correctness for doll	1-5	
Lashes	1-10	
Eyebrows	1-10	
Lips	1-10	
	TOTAL	0
III. Workmanship	**20 Points**	
Body finish	1-5	
Eye cutting, setting or painting	1-5	
Mouth and teeth cutting if appropriate	1-5	
Smoothness and cleaning of bisque, warping	1-5	
	TOTAL	0
IV. Costume	**15 Points**	
Style, correct for doll's date	1-5	0
Fit, sewing, fabric choice	1-5	0
Underwear, shoes, socks	1-5	-2
	TOTAL	-2

POINTS LOST

OVERALL APPEARANCE	0
PAINTING	0
WORKMANSHIP	0
COSTUME	-2
TOTAL POINTS DEDUCTED	-2
SCORE (100 - Points Deducted) = Score	98

Entry Number 56

Class 6

Division Professional

Category

Award Blue

Comments: The doll is a wonderful and true reproduction. I do believe you could have found a handmade copy of a Marque shoe pattern. Marque shoes are in the Dollmakers Workbook French Dolls on page 69.

90-100	Blue Ribbon
75-89	Red Ribbon
65-74	White Ribbon
Below 64	Exhibitor's Ribbon

Highest scores will receive Rosettes for Best of Class. Trophies will be awarded for Best of Show.

Explanation of Seeley Educational Doll Judging System

Each doll is to be judged individually on its own merits. If a doll is excellent, it deserves a blue ribbon regardless of how many excellent dolls there are. If a doll is good, it will receive a red ribbon; fair, a white ribbon. If the doll is poor, no ribbon will be awarded even if it is the only doll in its class.

Remember, the Seeley Educational Doll Judging System is meant to encourage dollmaking and educate the dollmakers as to where and how they can improve their dollmaking.

MILDRED SEELEY'S **EDJS** EDUCATIONAL DOLL JUDGING SYSTEM

Reproduction Dolls

To customize this form, place the name of your show here... ...then photocopy.

		POINTS DEDUCTED
I. Overall appearance	**30 Points**	
Similarity to antique doll	1-15	______
Costume, wig and shoes appropriate for doll	1-5	______
Proportion of head to body	1-10	______
	TOTAL	______
II. Painting	**35 Points**	
Cheek and other blending, smoothness and correctness for doll	1-5	______
Lashes	1-10	______
Eyebrows	1-10	______
Lips	1-10	______
	TOTAL	______
III. Workmanship	**20 Points**	
Body finish	1-5	______
Eye cutting, setting or painting	1-5	______
Mouth and teeth cutting if appropriate	1-5	______
Smoothness and cleaning of bisque, warping	1-5	______
	TOTAL	______
IV. Costume	**15 Points**	
Style, correct for doll's date	1-5	______
Fit, sewing, fabric choice	1-5	______
Underwear, shoes, socks	1-5	______
	TOTAL	______

90-100	Blue Ribbon
75-89	Red Ribbon
65-74	White Ribbon
Below 64	Exhibitor's Ribbon

Highest scores will receive Rosettes for Best of Class.
Trophies will be awarded for Best of Show.

POINTS LOST

OVERALL APPEARANCE	______
PAINTING	______
WORKMANSHIP	______
COSTUME	______
TOTAL POINTS DEDUCTED	______
SCORE (100 - Points Deducted) = **Score**	______

Entry Number ______________

Class ______________

Division ______________

Category ______________

Award ______________

Comments:

____

____

____

____

____

____

____

____

____

____

Explanation of Seeley Educational Doll Judging System

Each doll is to be judged individually on its own merits. If a doll is excellent, it deserves a blue ribbon regardless of how many excellent dolls there are. If a doll is good, it will receive a red ribbon; fair, a white ribbon. If the doll is poor, no ribbon will be awarded even if it is the only doll in its class.

Remember, the Seeley Educational Doll Judging System is meant to encourage dollmaking and educate the dollmakers as to where and how they can improve their dollmaking.

Exhibit card for this antique should read: Bru, Bru Jne 9, c. 1885, on all leather body including feet, 25".

Individual Exhibit Cards

Antique, collectible, reproduction and sometimes modern dolls must have a card of explanation *exhibited* with each doll. This card should be typed or printed by the doll owner. These should be done carefully in black ink so they can be read from some distance. The card will tell the judges the markings on the doll and the approximate date the doll was made.

The card will be exhibited along with the doll as part of the exhibit to increase the public's general knowledge about the doll. It will include where and how the doll is marked, and other pertinent information that they cannot see on the doll.

A 3 x 5 card will work well. These can also be printed and mailed out with the registration forms. All the cards should be uniform to make a better looking exhibit. Owners' names should not be on the card. Comments on the card should tell anything unusual concerning the doll, regarding construction, history or mechanism.

Above, a Millie winner. Note how the card folds up to cover the name.

Antique

Exhibitor's # ______________ Class ______________
Maker of doll ______________
Head markings ______________
Body markings ______________
Circa (approximate date) ______________
Repairs, damages ______________
Photo of antique doll in ______________ page ______
Comments: ______________

Reproduction

Exhibitor's # ______________
Class ______________
*Professional ______________
*Non-Professional ______________
*Senior ______________
*Novice ______________
*Other ______________
Head markings ______________
Mold Co. ______________
Circa of antique doll ______________
Photo of antique doll in ______________ page ______

* Used on the exhibit card only when there is a very large show. *Professional* refers to anyone who teaches or sells dolls. *Non-Professional* or hobbyist is a person who makes dolls for fun. *Senior Citizen* is anyone over 60. *Novice* is a first-time competitor and can only be entered once in this category.

Right, 20" marked Jullien in excellent condition with excellent bisque. She has an old mohair wig.

1ST
REGION 8
CHATTANOOGA, TENN
MAY 11, 1963

Each group must be separated into a division of the doll classes and ribbons awarded accordingly.

Some exhibitor's cards have a folded section where their name will go. After they put their name on the card, the name section is folded and sealed down, hiding the exhibitor's name. After all the judging is completed and the dolls are displayed for exhibit, the name is revealed.

Exhibitor cards are to be made out for every doll exhibited. This is one of the most important features of my educational judging plan. No matter how large or small the show, there must be exhibitor cards.

The reproduction doll exhibitor will have to research her doll in order to complete the exhibitor card. And in the process, the dollmaker will become more knowledgeable about her doll, perhaps even learning some of her doll's history. (It always surprises me when I find a student with a lovely reproduction doll, and then find out she doesn't even know the mold's origin.) She may also find several photos of dolls like her own which might help her to critically examine her painting of the doll. It's unfortunate that some students just paint dolls without doing research. Doing the necessary research for the exhibitor's card can sometimes prepare the dollmaker for the judge's criticism. This is all part of the Seeley Educational Doll Judging System.

The exhibitor's card becomes especially important after the doll has been judged and displayed for the public to view.

This is how exhibitors' cards work at a small show.

Far left, creative Diane Arneson won a rosette in Australia for this doll. She researched the costuming and embroidered this raw silk coat. Left, generally speaking, exact reproductions are harder to make and take more skill. Here Jamie Englert has copied the costume and everything as exactly as possible.

Exhibit cards are also vital for the judges. They provide the necessary information concerning the doll, saving guesswork and making the judging more accurate, as well as speeding up the judging.

In regards to antique dolls the exhibit card is vital. It forces the person exhibiting to research her doll. After this exercise, she is more apt to get the doll in the right class or category.

Since very few attending the show would recognize all the antique dolls, the exhibit cards help to educate the public and make the show more exciting.

This doll shows the creative talents of Diane Arneson.

Marking Competition Dolls

It is essential for the competition that the doll be made by the person entering the doll. Therefore, dolls should be carefully checked as they are entered. This entails lifting the hair, taking off or lifting the tape to expose the initials of the dollmaker and the year in which the doll was made. The judges must not see these identifying markings, so they should be checked before the competition begins.

If there are no markings, or the initials are not those of the exhibitor, the doll is disqualified.

Now, in order to simplify this procedure for all competitions, large and small all over the country, one simple and effective type of marking should be standard (see figure). If all dollmakers who intend to compete will follow this standard procedure, it will save time and effort for the officials. It will also eliminate the need to take off the wigs or clothing while locating the identification markings.

Instructions for marking all would-be competition dolls: Incise the doll with your initials on the middle of the back of the neck. Incise the four numerals of the year. Do all your competition dolls this way.

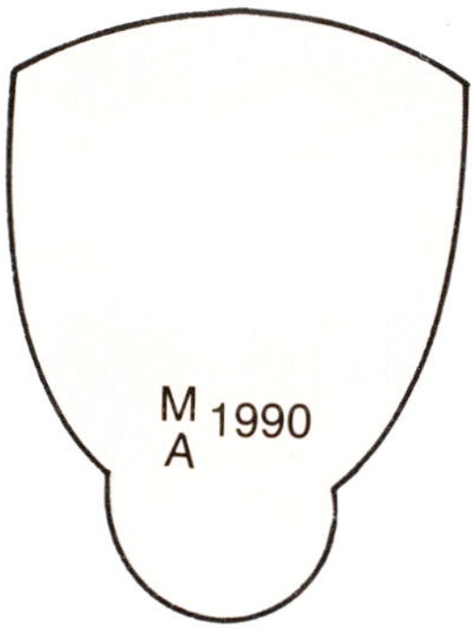

Send this information with your first show or competition announcement. This standardizing information should be spread to all studios and dollmakers. It will save confusion worldwide.

This 25" antique doll is marked Eden Be'be'.

Dolls Not Made as Reproductions

In several shows across the country, we found a special class added for dollmakers doing their own thing—not making true reproduction dolls that are created in the image of the antique. One show called these "Novelties," another, "Not Reproductions," and one, "Do Your Own Thing."

This class can be very charming. But if the dolls are just poorly painted dolls from antique doll molds, it is better to leave the class out. There could be a special theme for these dolls such as, fairy tale characters,

Most collectors would not recognize this French Pan doll by Henri Delcroix made around 1887.

clowns, brother and sister pairs, Christmas characters and so on. These dolls can add a great deal of charm and something different to the whole show. There probably should be specifications for these dolls, regarding size, number in groups and perhaps even molds.

This type of doll will require special judging. The judging sheet will have to be a cross between reproduction dolls and artist dolls. Here we must be careful to give full credit for originality and creativity.

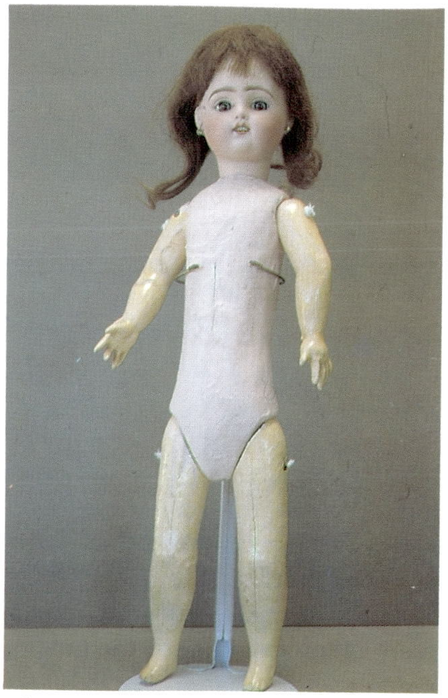

Above, rare 18" LeConte made in Paris c. 1890. Wouldn't it be nice if we could always see right through the clothing to judge the quality of the doll?

Judges Meet the Exhibitors

After all the judging is finished and the show draws to a close, the judges and the judging system's real test will come.

Those people with pale ribbons will want a further explanation about why their ribbon wasn't blue or how they can improve before the next show.

The judges, the chairman of the judging department, or someone knowledgeable in the new system of judging should meet with these competitors on a one-to-one basis. The explanation should be short, very friendly, but to the point. It should always encourage and attempt to create an incentive to improve. Along with the explanation, some suggestions for where to find some helpful information is important.

If the painting is very bad, talk to the dollmaker about using good quality brushes. If the doll is incorrectly painted, tell her to consult the antique doll's photograph. If it looks like she needs practice, tell her. And in some cases, if you suspect that good instruction was lacking, suggest a change of teachers or some book study on that type of doll. If the doll is very good, but could be improved with better painting, suggest a seminar with an expert.

The judge should check to see if all the points came off in one area. For example, if they were all taken off for clothing, the doll was probably too overdressed. The doll may have been "buried" in ruffles that didn't complement its face well. If this is the case, suggest that she study the book, *Doll Costuming*, which explains how the dolls were originally dressed.

If all of the doll's workmanship looks hurried, do not hesitate to note that the doll needs more time and effort.

Some standard responses can be used, such as: "You haven't been making dolls for as long as most of the other dollmakers here;" or "On these tiny dolls, try working with a magnifying glass;" or "You may do much better when you have a kiln and can work at your own speed." As you continue to work with the beginners, you will become better and better at explaining your judging decisions. Remember, it is essential that the dollmakers go home happy, more informed, and with a determination to win a blue ribbon next time.

Right, most Brus are of a fine quality, but not all. This 34" Bru is perfection.

brocade on the outside of the sleeves from the elbow up is in shreds. The rest of the dress is in good condition. Other dolls have been picked up by the waist and you can see the discoloration from handling.

I have an easy solution for this potential problem during judging. I first saw judges at work judging quilts in Pennsylvania and they were wearing white gloves. While judging or handling photographs, white gloves are always worn. I believe white gloves should be worn to judge dolls, all dolls.

My son is the head of the art department at Wesleyan University in Connecticut. I asked him about gloves. We got some and we have been using them for years in our judging seminars.

Note: Inexpensive, thin and disposable gloves may be purchased from: Lion Mills Inc., 11405 Rojas Dr., El Paso, TX 79936, (915) 594-3311.

A lovely Halopeau in an original dress and bonnet. Use white cotton gloves to move or handle her.

Right, in practice sessions, the judges had to judge a row of A.T.'s. This was a good experience in identification, but this situation probably wouldn't happen in a real judging situation, because A.T.'s are too scarce.

Rare 225 Jumeau Character in original silk taffeta dress and hat. You can see that costumes like this should be treated gently and only touched with a gloved hand.

Suggestions for Antique Doll Judges

1. Reread the description of the class you are judging. If there is anything you do not understand, ask the chairman.
2. All dolls will be judged, even if there is only one in the class.
3. Dolls will be judged against the ideal, not against the other dolls exhibited in that class.
4. Check to see if the dolls have the correct number on your table.
5. Record the doll's award.
6. Write suggestions and constructive criticism on judging sheets.
7. Be generous. Where there is indecision, give the next highest ribbon. Always have in mind the exhibitor and the show's goal to educate the viewing public.
8. Handle dolls as little as possible.
9. Trust the exhibitor's card, but have sharp eyes and watch dates.
10. Have reference books handy.
11. Be relaxed and enjoy the experience.
12. Keep your commentary objective.
13. Never openly criticize other judges.
14. Do not judge a class in which you have a doll exhibited.
15. Judge the dolls along with the other judges with a spirit of compatibility and cooperation.
16. Don't leave the judging room or talk to anyone on the outside until the head judge or chairman has released you.
17. Always wear white cotton gloves while handling antique dolls.
18. In a category, such as Bru dolls from 10" to 25", do not give more points to the largest doll just because she is the larger. The small dolls are to be considered equal to the large dolls as far as size is concerned.

MILDRED SEELEY'S EDJS EDUCATIONAL DOLL JUDGING SYSTEM

Antique and Collectible Dolls

To customize this form, place the name of your show here... ...then photocopy.

Note: With antique or collectible doll judging, it is essential to know what is original or authentic. For example, did this doll have head markings, body markings or none at all? The following guidelines are meant to be applied only where appropriate.

		POINTS DEDUCTED
I. Rarity	**35 Points**	
Seldom seen because few were made or few have lasted	1-20	______
The older the doll in that class the more points	1-15	______
	TOTAL	______
II. Doll's Condition	**25 Points**	______
Look for wear on face, body and wig	1-10	______
Replaced, repaired, reproduction parts	1-5	______
Cracks, repair or touch-up on bisque or eyes	1-5	______
Sleep eyes, flirty eyes, etc. in working condition	1-5	______
	TOTAL	______
III. Authenticity	**15 Points**	______
Head marking; note, not a reproduction	1-5	______
Body marking, labels	1-5	______
Shoes or clothing markings	1-5	______
	TOTAL	______
IV. Originality	**25 Points**	______
Original dress or appropriate attire	1-10	______
Original shoes, socks, etc.	1-5	______
Original wig	1-5	______
Original hat or bonnet	1-5	______
(Full points awarded for originals only; less for contemporary; even less for modern.)		
	TOTAL	______

90-100	Blue Ribbon
75-89	Red Ribbon
65-74	White Ribbon
Below 64	Exhibitor's Ribbon

Highest scores will receive Rosettes for Best of Class.
Trophies will be awarded for Best of Show.

Explanation of Seeley Educational Doll Judging System

Each doll is to be judged individually on its own merits. If a doll is excellent, it deserves a blue ribbon regardless of how many excellent dolls there are. If a doll is good, it will receive a red ribbon; fair, a white ribbon. If the doll is poor, no ribbon will be awarded even if it is the only doll in its class.

Remember, the Seeley Educational Doll Judging System is meant to encourage doll collecting and educate the collectors as to where and how they can improve their collections.

POINTS LOST

RARITY	______
DOLL'S CONDITION	______
AUTHENTICITY	______
ORIGINALITY	______
TOTAL POINTS DEDUCTED	______
SCORE (100 - Points Deducted) = **Score**	______

Entry Number ______________

Class ______________

Division ______________

Category ______________

Award ______________

Comments:

____

____

____

____

____

____

____

____

____

____

Judging Your First Antique Doll

So you have never judged an antique doll before. Let us start by judging this one together. You mark the judging sheet. The following will be a guideline for judging antique dolls. Even this pattern will not do for all antique dolls, because there is such a variety and seldom are there two dolls exactly alike. Only after you really know antique dolls, can you feel confident jumping into judging. Practice always helps.

This doll is entered in the Antique German Character Dolls class, 15" to 24".

Here we are working with a very expensive German character doll. How expensive you want to know—well anywhere from $4,000 to $6,000. This you should know is one of the largest of the Fanys ever made. It is a coveted doll among doll collectors.

Now if you were judging by yourself, how would you decide about rarity? Think: How many times have you seen the doll? How many times has she been listed in the auction catalogs? Did you know that she was made and sold to one individual firm? This low production makes her rare.

Exhibit Card

Exhibitor's # 321 Class D
Maker Armand Marseille
Head marking Fany 231 DRMR 248/1 A5M
Body marking None
Circa 1912
Repairs, damages Upper legs replaced
Comments: This is a seldom found closed-mouth German doll.

Fany's markings.

Fany, 20", marked 231.

Fany has an open-close mouth and sleep eyes.

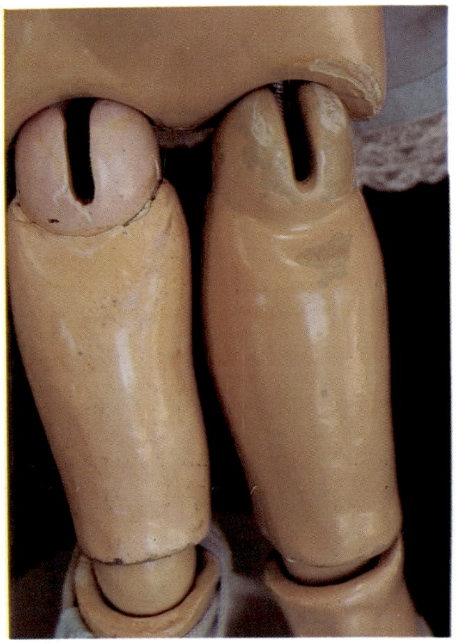

Fany's replaced upper legs.

I see the doll isn't one you know. Under ordinary judging circumstances you should quickly look her up in *Cieslik's German Doll Encyclopedia.*

The card told you the doll was made in 1912. This is the time when character dolls were starting to be produced. In a class with Simon & Halbig and Kammer and Reinhardt dolls, this doll could be younger or older, but only by a year or so.

I see you gave her all 35 points. Good. We will go on to study the doll's condition. Remember she was a toy 79 years ago. We will take this into consideration.

The face and head are perfect. The wig is somewhat thin in places, but overall it is good. The body is excellent with all the fingers on and with a little wear—but oops why doesn't the doll stand better? The card says she has replaced upper legs. This I feel should be investigated. With cotton gloves on we very carefully examine the legs. We find replaced upper legs. But both of the legs are left upper legs. No wonder she doesn't stand the way she should.

We will take off 5 points here; this is a bad replacement. The doll's eyes are sleep eyes and they work. Under authenticity we note that the doll's head is well marked and marked Fany. (There were some Fanys that were not marked.) The body is not marked and we know Armand Marseille, the maker, did not mark bodies. There is no mark on the shoes or clothing.

Down to originality. The dress is not original, but is very appropriate and charming—it fits and the color is good. We must take off 2 points. The shoes are German, but seem a little too large for the doll—probably not original. Take off 1 point. Fany doesn't have a bonnet on in any of her photos.

On the whole this is a very charming and good doll. In spite of the two upper left legs, she is a blue ribbon winner.

MILDRED SEELEY'S EDJS EDUCATIONAL DOLL JUDGING SYSTEM

Antique and Collectible Dolls

To customize this form, place the name of your show here... *...then photocopy.*

Note: With antique or collectible doll judging, it is essential to know what is original or authentic. For example, did this doll have head markings, body markings or none at all? The following guidelines are meant to be applied only where appropriate.

		POINTS DEDUCTED
I. Rarity	**35 Points**	
Seldom seen because few were made or few have lasted	1-20	
The older the doll in that class the more points	1-15	
TOTAL		0
II. Doll's Condition	**25 Points**	
Look for wear on face, body and wig	1-10	
Replaced, repaired, reproduction parts	1-5	-5
Cracks, repair or touch-up on bisque or eyes	1-5	
Sleep eyes, flirty eyes, etc. in working condition	1-5	
TOTAL		-5
III. Authenticity	**15 Points**	
Head marking; note, not a reproduction	1-5	
Body marking, labels	1-5	
Shoes or clothing markings	1-5	
TOTAL		0
IV. Originality	**25 Points**	
Original dress or appropriate attire	1-10	-2
Original shoes, socks, etc.	1-5	-1
Original wig	1-5	
Original hat or bonnet	1-5	
(Full points awarded for originals only; less for contemporary; even less for modern.)		
TOTAL		-3

90-100	Blue Ribbon
75-89	Red Ribbon
65-74	White Ribbon
Below 64	Exhibitor's Ribbon

Highest scores will receive Rosettes for Best of Class.
Trophies will be awarded for Best of Show.

Explanation of Seeley Educational Doll Judging System
Each doll is to be judged individually on its own merits. If a doll is excellent, it deserves a blue ribbon regardless of how many excellent dolls there are. If a doll is good, it will receive a red ribbon; fair, a white ribbon. If the doll is poor, no ribbon will be awarded even if it is the only doll in its class.

Remember, the Seeley Educational Doll Judging System is meant to encourage doll collecting and educate the collectors as to where and how they can improve their collections.

POINTS LOST

RARITY	0
DOLL'S CONDITION	-5
AUTHENTICITY	0
ORIGINALITY	-3
TOTAL POINTS DEDUCTED	-8
SCORE (100 - Points Deducted) = Score	92

Entry Number ______
Class ______
Division ______
Category ______

Award Blue

Comments:
This is a wonderful collectors' doll. I believe a better leg replacement can be found.

All bisque dolls under 10". They are numbered left to right (1-4).

Small Dolls Under 10" Made Before 1930

MILDRED SEELEY'S EDJS EDUCATIONAL DOLL JUDGING SYSTEM

JUDGING EXERCISE

Small dolls, dolls under 10", come in so many different forms it is impossible to judge them together. These small dolls would include all bisque with joints, French or German, no joints, molded hair, wigs, and so on. Dollhouse dolls are also small dolls. Kewpies are small dolls. "Nodders" as well as bisque heads on composition bodies come in this group. These dolls must be set up in different classes. We find it difficult to make a judging sheet that will cover all little dolls. In this class we must mark the things that are appropriate for that group of dolls. We will not take off for things that do not apply.

Doll 3 is disqualified because it appears to be a reproduction of Little Beth, mold S403.

Pretend you are actually a judge and you are going to judge this group of all bisque dolls. These are typical of what might be exhibited at a small show. Read their exhibit cards. Mark their scores and award ribbons. This class calls for jointed all bisque dolls under 10" made before 1930. I will help you. We will call the dolls by their placement in the photo, starting from the left. Why not stop and judge these for yourself?

Ready? Start by giving all the dolls a quick going-over to be sure they all belong in this all bisque under 10" class made before 1930.

I see you already have a problem with doll number 3. I agree

Doll 1 doesn't even wear a dress and is in poor condition.

This close-up of Doll 2 shows her crossed eyes.

Does Doll 4's bonnet and dress seem appropriate?

with you; the doll must be disqualified. It appears to be made from mold S 403 from Seeley's in Oneonta, NY. (I made this mold from one of my dolls about 20 years ago.) Shove this doll to the back. Do not judge it.

You judge all the other dolls to be about the same age—made in the 20s.

You have been inspecting doll number 1. What did you find? I feel this is a poor doll. I had to take off for poor bisque, poor painting, sleep eyes are crossed and do not work, body and fingers chipped, material tied around the body of the doll is not a dress or costume. I came up with a score of 50. I did not give a ribbon. The first time I went over it I came up with even less. What did you find with doll number 2? She is not rare. Her bisque is good. She only has four joints. Her eyes are glass, crossed and do not sleep properly. Her painting is good, except for a spot on the lips. Under Condition, I marked off for touch-up over her right eye and rub mark on her nose. Her costume appears to be a commercial one from the 50s or 60s. Her wig appears to be original. I came up with a score of 72 for a white ribbon.

Doll 4 is not rare or very old. The quality of the bisque is fine. She has four joints only. Her glass eyes work. Her painting is excellent. I feel I must take off for the costume even though I know the old black silk dress may have been her first dress. But the dress and the baby bonnet do not seem appropriate. Minus 10 points. This doll is a blue ribbon winner.

I believe you have judged the doll correctly. The full length black silk dress was probably mother-made and decorated. The bonnet was also handmade. I do wonder if the dress had been made for an earlier, different type of doll. Perhaps even the bonnet was made for a baby doll.

None of these dolls were the super swivel-necked, many jointed, or rare dolls we hope to see exhibited in this class. In any show we must judge what is exhibited.

MILDRED SEELEY'S
EDJS
EDUCATIONAL
DOLL JUDGING SYSTEM

Small Dolls Under 10"

Made Before 1930

To customize this form, place the name of your show here... ...then photocopy.

		POINTS DEDUCTED
I. Rarity	**25 Points**	
Seldom seen	1-15	______
Age-older more points	1-10	______
	TOTAL	______
II. Construction	**20 Points**	
Quality of head and body material	1-5	______
Number of joints, including swivel neck. More joints more points.	1-5	______
Glass eyes, sleep eyes working, more points than painted eyes	1-5	______
Proportion of body and head	1-5	______
	TOTAL	______
III. Painting	**15 Points**	
Fine eyebrow and eyelash painting	1-10	______
Good face color	1-5	______
	TOTAL	______
IV. Condition	**20 Points**	
Cracks, chips, wear, touch up	1-10	______
Replaced or reproduction parts	1-10	______
	TOTAL	______
V. Costume	**20 Points**	
Original costume or appropriate attire	1-15	______
Original or appropriate wig	1-5	______
	TOTAL	______

90-100	Blue Ribbon
75-89	Red Ribbon
65-74	White Ribbon
Below 64	Exhibitor's Ribbon

Highest scores will receive Rosettes for Best of Class.
Trophies will be awarded for Best of Show.

Explanation of Seeley Educational Doll Judging System

Each doll is to be judged individually on its own merits. If a doll is excellent, it deserves a blue ribbon regardless of how many excellent dolls there are. If a doll is good, it will receive a red ribbon; fair, a white ribbon. If the doll is poor, no ribbon will be awarded even if it is the only doll in its class.

Remember, the Seeley Educational Doll Judging System is meant to encourage doll collecting and educate the collectors as to where and how they can improve their collections.

POINTS LOST

RARITY	______
CONSTRUCTION	______
PAINTING	______
CONDITION	______
COSTUME	______
TOTAL POINTS DEDUCTED	______
SCORE (100 - Points Deducted) = **Score**	______

Entry Number ______________

Class ______________

Division ______________

Category ______________

Award ______________

Comments:

____
____
____
____
____
____
____
____
____
____

*18" K*R 115. An old costume is always judged higher than an appropriate new costume on an antique doll.*

Modern Dolls

Many new collectors are interested in the "modern" dolls. Up until recently, these have not had a place in the doll shows.

The United Federation of Doll Clubs (UFDC) has set up a dating system for dolls to help to classify them. An antique doll is over 75 years old; a collectible doll is 35 to 75 years old; and a modern doll is 0 to 35 years old. Since rules are made to be broken, oftentimes we find bisque dolls made in the '20s exhibited with the antiques. It is the same with some fabric dolls. The reason for this inconsistency is that the categories are often set up according to materials, such as bisque or felt without dates.

Many of these dolls, even those from different companies were the same basic doll with the same head. The only difference is when the doll is wigged, dressed and boxed. The accessories that were sold with the doll might be taken into account also, such as hat, gloves and extra outfits. So we must judge the whole doll. But first, the doll must fit into a category. Usually these are arranged by specific dates, companies or perhaps doll size. Next, as with antique dolls, we must pick the oldest, the rarest or most unusual. Then, we must consider the condition. A "mint-in-box," unplayed with doll in original costume, wig and shoes is ideal.

If all the dolls are equal, it may be the accessories that make the doll a blue ribbon winner.

In the Seeley Educational Doll Judging System, it is not difficult to judge these dolls. Use a variation of the Antique and Collectible Judging form on page 49. We would still use the same judging theory— if there are two dolls with equal worth—we give them both the same color ribbon.

Great care should be taken in setting up classes for modern and collectible dolls. Have just a few select groups each year or the show will be swamped with modern dolls which will unbalance your show.

Boots Tyner, one of the top doll sculptors, gave me a "Portrait of Mil" done from a photograph of me at age five.

Modern Artist Doll Judges

A modern artist doll is a doll made by a doll artist from her own original idea and sculpture. Today, more people are having fun creating their own dolls than ever before.

To aid the judges, all doll artists exhibiting a doll must sign a statement that the doll is completely their original creation, meaning they sculpted the doll and no part was taken from an existing doll's mold. This eliminates any confusion about originality. Artists with dolls in medias other than bisque must also sign a statement similar to those required for soft dolls that states no commercial pattern was used, and the design is entirely their own. As for wood dolls, there would have to be a similar statement, ensuring that a wood copying machine was not used. For each doll in every category, there should be an appropriate signed statement, ensuring that each doll is the artist's original.

Hence, all dolls exhibited as an artist doll are assumed to be the work of the artist and the judge does not concern herself with the idea that it isn't.

To assess modern artist dolls, the judge needs some study of art and sculpture. She needs to know if the artistic impression as well as the workmanship is good, noting proportions and what is pleasing to the eye. The doll is judged as a piece of art. The costume and wig are considered part of the whole. Again, a better judge is someone who has made a few dolls. Sometimes, a good appreciation for dolls can substitute for an art background.

But the main thing to remember is to maintain an open mind and study each and every doll for its artistic interpretation, workmanship and appeal.

Artist dolls are some of the most difficult to judge fairly and potential judges should work at least two shows before judging on their own.

26" Hilda by Kestner is a favorite doll to reproduce.

Judging Your First Artist Doll

I know that you will make a good judge of artist dolls. You have an art background along with the basics of sculpture. I know that you have made reproduction dolls and are familiar with molds and processes. Remember you do not have to be concerned if the exhibitor really made the doll, because the exhibitor has already signed a form at registration stating she did.

Judging artist dolls is probably the most difficult of all doll judging. It calls for an unbiased, art-minded judge with enough experience and training to make sound judgments on the doll presented.

These artist dolls can vary so much that it is like judging apples and dogs together. But with my judging system, it is somewhat easier to judge these dolls, because each is judged individually on its own merits.

Let us judge this little 10" artist's production doll. We will use the score sheet for artist doll. We will judge the doll together. Be sure to say just what you are thinking. Any part you want to discuss—just tell me. Read the exhibit card before we begin.

Exhibit Card

Exhibitor's # 51 Class All-bisque Artists' Production

Comments: Each piece of this doll has been sculpted by the artist. No mold or existing doll or part was used. Molds were made from the original doll to make a limited edition of the doll.

This is 10" Oliver.

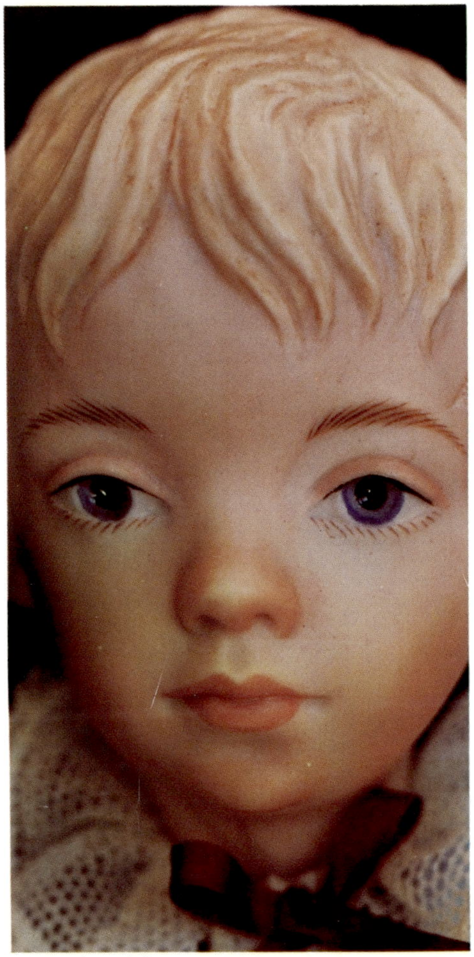

Oliver has delicate modeling.

Oliver's suit seems just perfect for him.

Under originality we have three of the most important judgments to make. What do you think about talent? I agree on giving him the full 10 points. Unlike any other doll—all 5 points—good. General appeal—it is a charming little doll.

Under overall appearance we look at the proportion of the head to body. It seems to be perfect. Next is proportion of hands and feet. I can see you have a problem with this. I agree with you the hands are too big or they lack child-like modeling or both. Can we deduct 2 points? I agree. The feet are great. The costume seems absolutely correct in all ways.

Now we will study the workmanship of this little doll. The bisque is beautifully smooth, the modeling of the face is perfection. The one-piece legs and arms fit well as does the swivel neck. I agree with you on these three points, the last point is not applicable.

Now for the painting. Just take a quick close look. Is there anything about the painting that bothers you? You like the painting. I feel it is very good too. The cheeks are perfectly blended though a little pale, eyebrows and lips are lovely. The eye treatment, intaglio with glaze is different, but exceptionally well done.

The costume is original, nice color for the doll. The fit and sewing are great.

MILDRED SEELEY'S EDJS EDUCATIONAL DOLL JUDGING SYSTEM

Artists Dolls

To customize this form, place the name of your show here... ...then photocopy.

		POINTS DEDUCTED
I. Originality	**25 Points**	
Shows creative talent	1-10	
Unlike any other doll	1-5	
General appeal	1-10	
TOTAL		0
II. General overall appearance	**20 Points**	
Proportion of head and body	1-10	
Proportion of hands and feet	1-5	-2
Costume appropriate for doll	1-5	
TOTAL		-2
III. Workmanship	**20 Points**	
Smoothness of bisque	1-5	
Symmetry of face	1-5	
Parts of doll fit together	1-5	
Eye cutting and fitting (if applicable)	1-5	
TOTAL		0
IV. Painting	**20 Points**	
Cheek and other blending	1-5	
Lashes, eyebrows and lips	1-5	
Eye painting (if applicable)	1-10	
TOTAL		0
V. Costume	**15 Points**	
Originality	1-5	
Color coordinated	1-5	
Fit and sewing	1-5	
TOTAL		0

90-100	Blue Ribbon
75-89	Red Ribbon
65-74	White Ribbon
Below 64	Exhibitor's Ribbon

Highest scores will receive Rosettes for Best of Class.
Trophies will be awarded for Best of Show.

POINTS LOST

ORIGINALITY	0
GENERAL APPEARANCE	-2
WORKMANSHIP	0
PAINTING	0
COSTUME	0
TOTAL POINTS DEDUCTED	-2
SCORE (100 - Points Deducted) = Score	98

Entry Number 51
Class Artist dolls
Category

Award Blue

Comments:
An interesting, well-made little doll. The judges felt the hands looked too old for the child.

Explanation of Seeley Educational Doll Judging System
Each doll is to be judged individually on its own merits. If a doll is excellent, it deserves a blue ribbon regardless of how many excellent dolls there are. If a doll is good, it will receive a red ribbon; fair, a white ribbon. If the doll is poor, no ribbon will be awarded even if it is the only doll in its class.

Remember, the Seeley Educational Doll Judging System is meant to encourage doll artists and educate the maker of original dolls as to where and how they can improve their dolls.

We're all done. What ribbon do you think the doll deserves? Does the point count come out the way you think it should? Yes. We both agree.

Judging an artist doll was not so hard after all. Now let me tell you about this wonderful little piece of sculpture. He is Oliver, a little English boy. He was sculpted by Nicholas Bramblle. He was made in 1982 in a limited edition production of 200. I believe the costume was made by Shirley Jones.

MILDRED SEELEY'S EDJS EDUCATIONAL DOLL JUDGING SYSTEM

Artists Dolls

To customize this form, place the name of your show here... ...then photocopy.

			POINTS DEDUCTED
I.	**Originality**	**25 Points**	
	Shows creative talent	1-10	______
	Unlike any other doll	1-5	______
	General appeal	1-10	______
		TOTAL	______
II.	**General overall appearance**	**20 Points**	
	Proportion of head and body	1-10	______
	Proportion of hands and feet	1-5	______
	Costume appropriate for doll	1-5	______
		TOTAL	______
III.	**Workmanship**	**20 Points**	
	Smoothness of bisque	1-5	______
	Symmetry of face	1-5	______
	Parts of doll fit together	1-5	______
	Eye cutting and fitting (if applicable)	1-5	______
		TOTAL	______
IV.	**Painting**	**20 Points**	
	Cheek and other blending	1-5	______
	Lashes, eyebrows and lips	1-5	______
	Eye painting (if applicable)	1-10	______
		TOTAL	______
V.	**Costume**	**15 Points**	
	Originality	1-5	______
	Color coordinated	1-5	______
	Fit and sewing	1-5	______
		TOTAL	______

POINTS LOST

ORIGINALITY	______
GENERAL APPEARANCE	______
WORKMANSHIP	______
PAINTING	______
COSTUME	______
TOTAL POINTS DEDUCTED	______
SCORE (100 - Points Deducted) = **Score**	______

Entry Number ______________

Class ______________

Category ______________

Award ______________

Comments:

____

____

____

____

____

____

____

____

____

90-100	Blue Ribbon
75-89	Red Ribbon
65-74	White Ribbon
Below 64	Exhibitor's Ribbon

Highest scores will receive Rosettes for Best of Class.
Trophies will be awarded for Best of Show.

Explanation of Seeley Educational Doll Judging System

Each doll is to be judged individually on its own merits. If a doll is excellent, it deserves a blue ribbon regardless of how many excellent dolls there are. If a doll is good, it will receive a red ribbon; fair, a white ribbon. If the doll is poor, no ribbon will be awarded even if it is the only doll in its class.

Remember, the Seeley Educational Doll Judging System is meant to encourage doll artists and educate the maker of original dolls as to where and how they can improve their dolls.

18" Bru Jne 7. Always check from a distance to see what the dress does for the doll, then check the sewing. This costume is by Suzanne Pirtle.

Costumes

During my judging experiences, costume judging, even with fine seamstresses as judges, turned out to be difficult. What to judge and how much to take off for each little infraction was hard to decide. The judges couldn't agree.

When I told one group of beginning judges that the costume they were judging was made by an 83-year-old woman, they wanted to forgive the loose threads hanging and the unmatched thread in another place. After some discussion, I convinced them that they were to judge the *costume* not the dressmaker.

I pointed out to the beginning judges that unless there were special classes for groups—such as 4-H clubs, senior citizens or some other group—all the costumes will be judged against the *same* standards.

There were certain things all the judges agreed upon. They all felt that finishing should be done by hand on parts that show, such as cuffs and hems. Seams could be machine stitched. The seamstress judges believed that zigzag was inappropriate for any part of the costume.

I felt that this particular group of judges failed to study the overall appearance of the costume. They didn't visualize what the costume did for the doll, which I believe is the most important aspect of the costume.

Another important factor to consider is whether the costume design was taken from, or was similar to what was originally on that particular doll. I believe more consideration should be placed on the appropriateness of the costume's design.

The quality of the sewing is very important, but not as important as the costume's overall appearance and design.

Exhibit cards should state what type of doll the dress is being displayed on so that the judges will know what type of dress the doll should be wearing. For example, Steiners often wore loose, lacy, and embroidered dresses with a bonnet-type hat. Jumeaux and Brus were known to wear formal, very pleated, elaborate but not frilly garments.

If an exhibitor intends to enter a costume for an antique doll, she *must* start with a doll that has no clothing—the doll must be nude. It must be completely costumed from the "skin" out including underclothing, shoes, socks, and bonnet if appropriate to the doll. *Small* accessories such as purses, flowers, or a tiny animal may be added to the whole composition. I do not believe in depreciating an antique doll by removing all or part of a doll's original clothing. Original clothing on dolls is sometimes as much as one-fourth their value.

Let's be as clear as possible. When dressing antique dolls, old material should be used wherever possible. It should end up with the "old look." Antiqued natural materials are acceptable. When dressing reproduction dolls, new materials of natural fibers should be used. The doll should look like the antique doll did when she was just purchased, fresh and new. Using antique lace with new material on a *reproduction* is *not* acceptable.

Right, 19" Tête Jumeau wearing a reproduction silk dress made by Angela Adams. The new material has been antiqued.

Judging the Costume of a Reproduction Doll for the First Time

This is your first time judging a reproduction costume using this score sheet. If you are a seamstress, I know you actually "judge" costumes every day of your life. I have seen your wonderful patterns on the market. I feel certain that this kind of judging will come naturally to you. You will be a careful, observant and fair-minded judge.

We will judge this first doll together, and you will see that it is done much the same way as you have been judging, with the exception that this one is scored.

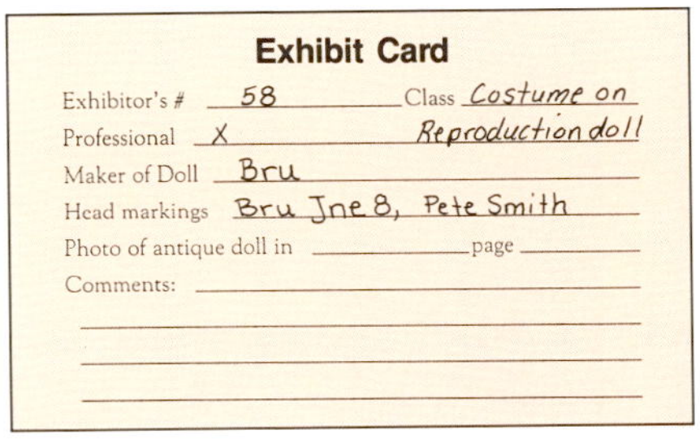
Exhibit Card

Exhibitor's # 58 Class Costume on Reproduction doll

Professional X

Maker of Doll Bru

Head markings Bru Jne 8, Pete Smith

Photo of antique doll in ______ page ______

Comments:

This Bru reproduction is entered in the costume class.

Note sewing on the front of her dress.

We will stand back and study the overall appearance of the costume in relationship to the doll. I like to think of the costume as a picture frame which draws attention and enhances the face.

Do you think the costume is proper for the doll? I see you are not altogether happy with the fabric. Look under section II of the judging sheet—we will take off for the cotton fabric there. The proportions are correct and the dress does enhance the doll. We will take nothing off here.

In section II, I know you feel as I do that the choice of polyester cotton fabric and inexpensive lace is not proper for a fine Bru reproduction. Minus 10 points. The color selection and coordination is well done, and it goes nicely with the doll. Her underclothing of bloomers with elastic and slip are too modern. She should wear a chemise, split drawers and petticoat. Take off 5 here.

In section III, you think the choice of pattern for the doll's date of 1885 is excellent. The fit is fine. The shoes, I believe are old shoes not made by the costumer. Brus wore socks. Minus 5.

Costume construction is really your "cup of tea." How would you judge this costume? The seams are well done but there is much machine stitching on the outside where the lace is attached. This would have been much nicer if done by hand. Minus 18.

I think the comments you have written on the bottom of the judging sheet are just right. Had the exhibitor read the directions and the book more carefully, she would have made the shoes, done the stitching on the outside of the dress by hand, and perhaps chosen a more appropriate fabric. His next exhibit will be a blue ribbon winner.

MILDRED SEELEY'S EDJS EDUCATIONAL DOLL JUDGING SYSTEM

Seamstress Competition
for Dressing a Reproduction Doll

To customize this form, place the name of your show here... ...then photocopy.

		Points Deducted
I. Overall appearance	**25 Points**	
Costume proper for doll	1-10	
Proportions correct	1-5	
Enhances the doll	1-10	
	TOTAL	0
II. Choice of fabric	**25 Points**	
New, but resembles old	1-10	-10
Color selection	1-5	
Color coordinated	1-5	
Underclothing proper	1-5	-5
	TOTAL	-15
III. Choice of pattern	**25 Points**	
Appropriate date for doll	1-10	
Proper fit	1-10	
Shoes and stockings correct date	1-5	-5
	TOTAL	-5
IV. Construction	**25 Points**	
Seams well done	1-5	-5
Hand sewing in proper places	1-10	-10
Stitching consistency	1-5	-3
Neatness-pressing	1-5	
	TOTAL	-18

90-100	Blue Ribbon
75-89	Red Ribbon
65-74	White Ribbon
Below 64	Exhibitor's Ribbon

Highest scores will receive Rosettes for Best of Class.
Trophies will be awarded for Best of Show.

Explanation of Seeley Educational Doll Judging System
Each doll is to be judged individually on its own merits. If a doll is excellent, it deserves a blue ribbon regardless of how many excellent dolls there are. If a doll is good, it will receive a red ribbon; fair, a white ribbon. If the doll is poor, no ribbon will be awarded even if it is the only doll in its class.

Remember, the Seeley Educational Doll Judging System is meant to encourage the costumer and educate the seamstress to improve their sewing and costuming.

POINTS LOST

OVERALL APPEARANCE	0
CHOICE OF FABRIC	-15
CHOICE OF PATTERN	-5
CONSTRUCTION	-18
TOTAL POINTS DEDUCTED	-38
SCORE (100 - Points Deducted) = Score	62

Entry Number 58
Class Costume on Reproduction
Division
Category Professional

Award No award

Comments:
This is a very fine reproduction Bru. It deserves a costume of fine material. Your color combination with her brown eyes is excellent. This same pattern could be done in silk taffeta and use handsewing any place it shows. Does you machine need adjusting?

MILDRED SEELEY'S
EDJS
EDUCATIONAL
DOLL JUDGING SYSTEM

Costume on Antique Dolls

To customize this form, place the name of your show here... ...then photocopy.

		POINTS DEDUCTED
I. Overall appearance	**25 Points**	
Costume proper for doll	1-10	______
Proportions correct	1-5	______
Enhances the doll	1-10	______
	TOTAL	______
II. Choice of fabric	**25 Points**	
Antique or old fabric	1-10	______
Color selection	1-5	______
Color coordinated	1-5	______
Underclothing proper	1-5	______
	TOTAL	______
III. Choice of pattern	**25 Points**	
Appropriate date for doll	1-5	______
Proper fit	1-5	______
Shoes and stockings correct date	1-5	______
Completeness of entry	1-10	______
	TOTAL	______
IV. Construction	**25 Points**	
Seams well done	1-5	______
Hand sewing in proper places	1-10	______
Stitching consistency	1-5	______
Neatness-pressing	1-5	______
	TOTAL	______

90-100	Blue Ribbon
75-89	Red Ribbon
65-74	White Ribbon
Below 64	Exhibitor's Ribbon

Highest scores will receive Rosettes for Best of Class.
Trophies will be awarded for Best of Show.

Explanation of Seeley Educational Doll Judging System

Each doll is to be judged individually on its own merits. If a doll is excellent, it deserves a blue ribbon regardless of how many excellent dolls there are. If a doll is good, it will receive a red ribbon; fair, a white ribbon. If the doll is poor, no ribbon will be awarded even if it is the only doll in its class.

Remember, the Seeley Educational Doll Judging System is meant to encourage the costumer and educate the seamstress to improve their sewing and costuming.

POINTS LOST

OVERALL APPEARANCE	______
CHOICE OF FABRIC	______
CHOICE OF PATTERN	______
CONSTRUCTION	______
TOTAL POINTS DEDUCTED	______
SCORE (100 - Points Deducted) = **Score**	______

Entry Number ______________

Class ______________

Division ______________

Category ______________

Award ______________

Comments:

____
____
____
____
____
____
____
____
____
____

24" Tete Jumeau in her original dress and umbrella. She lost her Jumeau shoes. Her card should indicate that the shoes are not original.

First Time Judging a Costume on an Antique Doll

You don't need to be the least bit nervous over judging costumes on antique dolls. I have seen the marvelous costumes you make for antique dolls, and I know how critical you are of your own work.

You have read the section on Judging Costumes and bits here and there on costume judging. Remember, we are not judging the doll, just the costume, and what the costume does for the doll. I have talked to

Exhibit Card

Exhibitor's # 6
Maker of doll Krammer and Reinhardt
Marks on the doll K*R 114
Circa 1912
Comments: I have made a little boy's one piece undergarment like an original on a K*R. I made the pattern for the suit myself by looking at a K*R's original one.

*Left, This K*R 114 HANS in new clothing made of old material.*

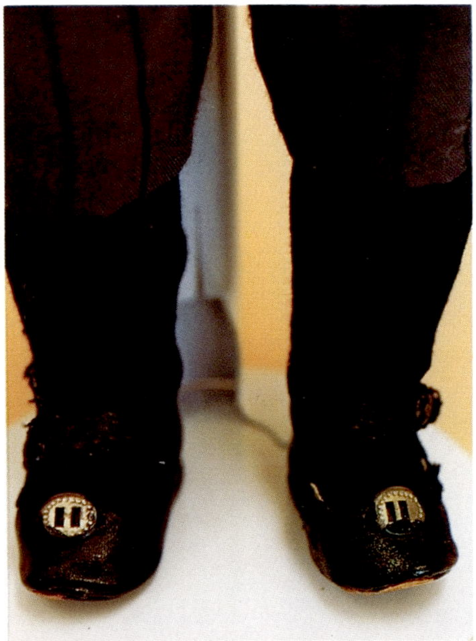

This exhibitor lost points on his shoes.

you about old parts of costumes, bonnets and the like—how important and valuable they are. So if there is something that is original to the doll like underwear or shoes, they are always left on the doll. We cannot depreciate the doll by removing original clothing, unless it is disintegrating or worthless. For the competition you must start with a doll that has no clothing left—a nude doll.

I believe the most important basic information a judge can have is a general knowledge of the type of clothing the different dolls wore when they were made. Knowledge as a seamstress comes second. Now we are going to judge a K*R's costume.

Stand back and look this guy over. You think his overall appearance is excellent. His costume is proper, proportions are correct and it enhances the doll. You wouldn't take off any points.

Under II the fabric is old pongee, old braid. His pants are made of very old striped blue cotton. His stockings are made from old wool stocking material. Colors are fine for a little boy. We can't see his underclothing but we believed what was on the card. You say you would have put either dark blue or black buttons on the pants. I would too. Minus 1.

Under III, on the card it tells us that the costumer drew her own pattern. This is the kind of play clothes worn by the K*Rs. His tiny silver antique whistle is a nice addition. His shoes appear to be antique—for this competition they must be made. Minus 2.

Under IV, the suit is well-constructed, the addition of the shirt pocket, pant's pocket, pant's fly are well done. Hand sewing and handmade buttons are excellent. No points off.

This little K*R HANS is costumed just right—play clothes were the costume of these dolls when they were produced. HAN's costume could rightly be called a reproduction costume as it was copied directly from another K*R.

MILDRED SEELEY'S EDJS EDUCATIONAL DOLL JUDGING SYSTEM

Costume on Antique Dolls

To customize this form, place the name of your show here... ...then photocopy.

		Points Deducted
I. Overall appearance	**25 Points**	
Costume proper for doll	1-10	
Proportions correct	1-5	
Enhances the doll	1-10	
	TOTAL	0
II. Choice of fabric	**25 Points**	
Antique or old fabric	1-10	
Color selection	1-5	
Color coordinated	buttons 1-5	-1
Underclothing proper	1-5	
	TOTAL	-1
III. Choice of pattern	**25 Points**	
Appropriate date for doll	1-5	
Proper fit	1-5	
Shoes and stockings correct date	1-5	
Completeness of entry	1-10	-2
	TOTAL	-2
IV. Construction	**25 Points**	
Seams well done	1-5	
Hand sewing in proper places	1-10	
Stitching consistency	1-5	
Neatness-pressing	1-5	
	TOTAL	0

90-100	Blue Ribbon
75-89	Red Ribbon
65-74	White Ribbon
Below 64	Exhibitor's Ribbon

Highest scores will receive Rosettes for Best of Class.
Trophies will be awarded for Best of Show.

Explanation of Seeley Educational Doll Judging System
Each doll is to be judged individually on its own merits. If a doll is excellent, it deserves a blue ribbon regardless of how many excellent dolls there are. If a doll is good, it will receive a red ribbon; fair, a white ribbon. If the doll is poor, no ribbon will be awarded even if it is the only doll in its class.

Remember, the Seeley Educational Doll Judging System is meant to encourage the costumer and educate the seamstress to improve their sewing and costuming.

POINTS LOST

OVERALL APPEARANCE	0
CHOICE OF FABRIC	-1
CHOICE OF PATTERN	-2
CONSTRUCTION	0
TOTAL POINTS DEDUCTED	-3
SCORE (100 - Points Deducted) = Score	97

Entry Number 6
Class Costume for antique doll
Division
Category non professional

Award Blue

Comments:
We found this outfit delightfully perfect for this German child doll. Wished you had made the shoes.

The Mechanics of Competition

Most doll shows have registration forms (see page 75) mailed in for all competitive entries at least three weeks to a month before the show. The reason for this is to know how many dolls and in which classes they will be exhibited. This way adequate space can be prepared for each group. Knowing how many dolls in each class will make hiring the correct number of judges easier too. It will also help while advertising the show.

It is important that this registration form for reproduction competition has a sentence or two that the dollmaker signs. It should be along these lines: *I have made and painted the doll(s) that I am entering in competition. Signed_______________.*

A similar form must be used for artists dolls, but this must cover the making of the doll more completely. Use something like this: *The doll(s) I am entering is completely of my own design, made without the use of an existing doll or mold or part thereof. The basic sculpture is my own as well as the finishing. It was not made in a seminar or with the aid of an instructor. Signed_________________.*

These forms take some pressure off the judges, because they will never have to consider whether or not the person made the doll herself. She has already signed a statement to that effect.

Somewhere in the directions or registration sheets, clearly state if the doll may have an accessory and how large it may be. Many shows allow accessories. State also that all dolls should have doll stands unless the doll is a baby doll with bent limbs that sits. Some shows prefer these baby dolls on stands as well as the other dolls.

Judging for Trophies

After all the preliminary judging is completed for all the classes, and all the rosette winners are set aside, the most difficult judging of all starts. This is the judging for the trophies—the winner of winners.

Some shows have several trophies, some have only one. It depends on the size of the show.

All the rosette winners are separated and from these the very best of show is selected. It is almost impossible to tell which of these dolls is best. At this level, we are judging dolls of all different types and sizes against one another. All of which probably rate a score of 100. The judging difficulty is not because these dolls are perfect. The difficulty is selecting a show winner from dolls which are not alike. They are not alike in size; in production difficulty; or in material or requirements for entry. This is not really judging; instead, it is making a selection that the judge or judging committee feels will best fill the bill of best overall doll. It's hard. There may be several you would like to pick. In this final selection there is no room for pettiness, prejudices, or personal likes or dislikes. This kind of selection takes time and must be carefully done.

Oftentimes there is more than one trophy. In some cases the miniature dolls have a trophy, original dolls have one, and the other dolls are grouped together. On the whole, trophies should be given where there are the most dolls in competition.

Sometimes there are special awards given just for certain classes. Other times companies give trophies for some class of dolls that they are especially interested in or wish to purchase for advertising. Often money awards or gift certificates are awarded besides the rosettes and trophies.

Trophy winners are selected from the rosette winners from all the classes.

Exhibit Committee and Judges Cooperate

Judges and exhibit committees must work together both before and after the show to make the Seeley Educational Doll Judging System really work. The idea is to have a successful show, one in which the onlookers as well as the exhibitors feel they have been inspired and learned something. This can only happen with trained judges working with the exhibit committee.

We still find at many shows across the country that untrained judges are called a day or two in advance of the show. They go in and judge the dolls in an hour before the show opens. This is not good or adequate judging. The show would be better off without judging.

You can easily see that cooperation is necessary to have the committee hire all trained judges, to have standardized judging sheets printed, to require exhibitor's cards for each doll, and to have the original doll artist sign an "I made it" statement.

One of the big problems in the shows today is the marking of reproduction dolls. This marking should be standardized for the shows and exhibitors told many months ahead. This will simplify and speed up the acceptance of dolls at the receiving desk. (See page 41.)

Exhibitors of all kinds need to know ahead of time how the doll is going to be judged. Here is where the Seeley Educational Doll Judging System needs to be publicized—before the show—before people decide not to enter their dolls.

Many things need to be decided ahead of time on the judging and setting up of classes. Judging score sheets need to be publicized.

Judges and committee must see eye-to-eye and work together. When judging is over, they should meet to discuss any problems or oversights.

Shows that have been running a long time and have their problems built-in will find it hardest to change. There can always be a period of transition where things are changed a few at a time. Greater success will be achieved if everything is changed to the Seeley Educational Doll Judging System all at once, and shows advertise that the system will be used.

As time goes on and more and more shows are set up under this system, judges will find their work easier.

BEBE

Doll Exhibitor's Information

- A total of ______ dolls may be entered by one person in each area, including reproduction and antique groups.
- Enter only one doll in a class unless it calls for pairs or groups.
- All entries must have exhibitor cards.
- The dollmaker's name must not show on the doll. Cover it with tape.
- Dolls should have stands that will hold them securely.
- Accessories are not judged and should not be included unless they are the original box or accessory. Or, the class permits accessories to be included with the exhibit.
- Note: New clubs or groups may want to be a little more lenient with their first few shows.
- **Previous blue ribbon winners may be entered in a class for "Blue Ribbon Winners" only.**
- Exhibitors must pick up their own dolls after showing a copy of the exhibitor's registration.

Insuring Dolls in Competition

At the large doll conventions, such as the UFDC, the dolls placed in competition are insured. After the entry form is filled out with a list of the dolls to be placed in competition, give the class number, the doll's description and the insurance evaluation.

I might add here that many owners of antique dolls have their dolls covered with "Fine Arts Policies," which are riders on their home insurance policies. This way the dolls are also covered during transit to and from the shows.

Small doll shows cannot afford to insure the dolls exhibited. This makes it a bit chancy for exhibitors. Usually a sentence is added at the bottom of the entry form stating there is no insurance. All exhibitors should sign something similar to the following:

The doll show committee will in all instances take the best possible care of my doll to prevent damage or theft, but the show carries no insurance and cannot be held responsible. ______________________

(exhibitor's signature)

Besides insurance, larger shows keep security guards on duty while the room is open. Most also have night guards staying in the rooms while it is closed to the public.

In small shows as well as large shows, a few club members can volunteer to stand guard to protect the dolls from damage. These people should be rotated so that they do not become too tired.

Left, 24" Jumeau Character without numbers.

29" Pan doll by Henri Delcroix. The ribbons belong to the doll and are usually pinned to the doll when she is sold.

Standardizing Award Ribbons

The color of award ribbons should be consistent worldwide for the main awards. This makes the viewing more educational for the public and easier for the contestants.

It has been a tradition for hundreds of years that the blue ribbon stands for an excellent product; the red ribbon stands for a good product; and the white ribbon stands for a fair product.

Beyond this point any colors can be used. Many use tri-colored red, white and blue rosettes for their Best of Class. This is often referred to as the "Tri-Color Award." Others choose royal purple or gold for their rosettes to denote the greatness of the award. Some just have larger ribbons made up in these colors to designate the award. Other groups make their large ribbons and rosettes in glamorous colors of pink, lavender or green. Some even match or coordinate ribbons with table covers or color schemes of the show.

Playing with colors can add to the whole look of the show *but* it is important that you maintain the blue, red and white awards for the general award system.

Ribbons should be printed with the name of the show, the place and the year. If more than one show is held a year, then add a designation such as "Fall," "Spring," or the date.

A ribbon without this information is of little value to the doll artist or antique doll collector. Remember, prize dolls are usually sold with their ribbons attached. The ribbon serves as a record for both the doll and its owner.

The color blue represents the highest honor in all fields of endeavor. Blue was supposedly used because the sky is the home of the gods.

Care and Feeding of Judges

Consider the judges very special people who need a little tender care while they carry out their responsibilities.

If a judge is coming in from a long distance and is flying, see that she is met and delivered to her hotel. If she is driving, be sure she has a parking space and gets a warm greeting.

The judges should be provided with runners to carry dolls from room to room, if necessary. Most judges are given an assistant or judge-in-training who marks the score sheets and writes in the judge's comments. This speeds up the whole judging process.

It is also good to provide the judge with a little nourishment as the hours wear on. There's nothing like a hot cup of coffee or tea and a cookie. If the judging lasts through lunch or dinner, be sure to plan meals. Either have meals brought in or take the judges out to a convenient and quick place to eat.

Before the judge is discharged, be sure no dolls or group of dolls have been missed. Trophy judging should be done last.

Give the judge the same courteous treatment after the judging is finished. Be sure she gets back to the airport or hotel and is not left stranded in the midst of the doll show confusion. You may need her many times again.

Unusual old paper mache with curls around her face and a snood in the back. Her eye painting is unusually fine. Her arms and boots are red leather. Her dress is purple silk with a red print. She has never been exhibited. I have never found this doll in a book nor have I ever seen a duplicate of her.

Setting Up Categories for Competition

Category selection must be carefully done. Categories must have exact definitions and accurate terminology, which will help to eliminate much of the confusion for the exhibitor. It also narrows down the types that are to be judged together. It helps the judges, but more importantly, it helps the people viewing the dolls to understand exactly why a certain doll is judged for a blue ribbon, etc.

With everything spelled out, few dolls would be placed in the wrong category. Where necessary, give size; dates or period; marks or no marks; woman; child; baby; wig or molded hair. Anything to make the category clear, concise and complete.

One of the biggest problems with small doll shows is entering dolls in the wrong category. Oftentimes it is the exhibit committee's fault for not carefully working out the categories ahead of time.

For instance, the two categories below overlap and may cause the exhibitor confusion, because they are so much alike.

Class IV German; child character type; under 16"; marked; with painted eyes; 1900-1920; no Googlies.

Class V German; boys under 16"; marked; with painted eyes; 1900-1920.

Would you know which category to put a boy doll into, IV or V? Probably not. This sort of thing happens all the time when not enough care is taken while setting up the categories.

Exhibitors who are not familiar with the category terms should have a telephone number of an expert whom they can call for help. It would also help if exhibitors were allowed to change categories while presenting their dolls for exhibit, if the expert in charge of entries suggests that the doll is entered in the wrong category.

The following list is a guideline that will help you while setting up categories.

1. Indicate head materials, such as china, bisque, cloth, celluloid, wax or wood.
2. Indicate body material as cloth, leather, composition, celluloid, wood or other.
3. Indicate whether the exhibit is to be a man, woman, child, or fashion lady.
4. Indicate if the exhibit can have pairs or groups.
5. In some instances, indicate whether the eyes are painted or glass; mouths are open or closed; hair is wigged or molded.

Opposite page, 32" doll marked E D by Denamur. Large dolls like this are seldom exhibited because of their size.

6. Most exhibits need a size range, so that large dolls and miniatures are not competing.
7. Give dates in 20-year periods, such as 1890-1910. On the very old dolls, this is sometimes given as "before" such and such a date.
8. In some instances, as with Parian, you may need to indicate "with decoration" or "without decoration," because these two could be hard to judge together.
9. With lady dolls, you may want to indicate the type of arms and legs as wood or leather; or leather bodies with bisque hands and feet.
10. Dolls such as Kewpies are usually in a category all by themselves.
11. Indicate if accessories are considered or should be left off.
12. Indicate if the doll is to be on an appropriate doll stand or "sat" as with a baby doll.

Category Examples

There are hundreds of categories and variations for dolls used in shows and conventions. Here is a list from which you may draw ideas.

Baby dolls - cloth body, flange neck or shoulder head
Baby dolls - swivel neck, composition body
Baby dolls - painted eyes
German children dolls - glass eyes
German children dolls - painted eyes
German children dolls - boy dolls
German children dolls - 18" and over
French children dolls - composition body under 17"
French children dolls - composition body over 17"
French children dolls - boy dolls
French children dolls - leather body
Jumeau children dolls - under 20"
Lady dolls - Gibson Girl and others
French Fashion - leather body
Mechanical dolls on musical stands
Mechanical dolls - large bodies
Googlies - over 8"
Googlies - bisque under 8"
Doll house dolls
All bisque dolls under 10"
Modern dolls - such as Joyce Wolf's molds and others
Novelty dolls - not true reproductions
French reproductions

Opposite page, 15" marked Rohmer. A blue ribbon doll that was exhibited under "French Fashion with painted eyes."

25" French mechanical marked F.G. Most people do not exhibit their mechanicals, because it gets the mechanism out of order.

German reproductions
The Milettes
Your sales table
Previous blue ribbon winners (which make a fine display)
Seamstress costume, by owner or maker
German children dolls in white to show hand sewing

Antique Categories

French Bisque

French fashion, cloth or leather body, leather limbs, 14" or over
French fashion, cloth or leather body, non-leather limbs, 14" or over
French fashion, cloth or leather body, leather limbs, under 14"
French fashion, cloth or leather body, non-leather limbs, under 14"
French fashion, wood or part wood bodies
Jumeau children, marked or unmarked, under 18"
Jumeau children, marked or unmarked, 18" or over
Bru, marked or unmarked, including Brevete', under 18"
Bru, marked or unmarked, including Brevete', 18" and over
All other French children marked as to maker, under 18"
All other French children marked as to maker, 18" and over
All French children not marked as to maker, under 18"
All French children not marked as to maker, 18" and over
Steiner children, any size
F.G. children, any size
All French children with open mouths
French character with exaggerated expressions

German Bisque

German children, marked K*R, with glass eyes
German children, marked K*R, with painted eyes
German children, marked S & H and numbers only
German children, marked Simon and Halbig and numbers only
German children, marked Heubach, with glass eyes
German children, marked Heubach, with painted eyes
German children, marked J.D.K.
German children, marked Armand Marseille
German children, marked as to maker other than above
German children not marked as to maker, but may include numbers, letters and/or country of origin marks
German children with glass Googly eyes
German children with painted Googly eyes
German lady dolls with adult body, any maker

Above, a group of so-called Milliner's Models. Paper mache heads, wood hands and feet with leather body. Judge these by their hair-dos and condition. Don't expect perfection in an 1830-1850 doll, but they are inexpensive and fun to collect.

This wood doll has two pieces of clothing left—a dress and an apron. Note the crude joints. In a group of wood dolls she might take the rosette. Her age and good condition are pluses. She is 17" tall.

German man dolls, with molded and/or painted facial characteristics, designating an adult male
German baby dolls, with painted eyes, bent limb body
German baby dolls, with glass eyes, bent limb body

All Bisque Dolls

All bisque over 8"
All bisque with molded shoes and molded hair, under 8"
All bisque with bare feet, jointed at shoulder and hip only (may have swivel neck)
All bisque with bare feet or molded shoes, jointed at knees and/or elbows
All bisque with molded clothing, but not molded hats
All bisque with molded hats or bonnets
All bisque with molded facial hair, such as beards, mustaches, side burns

Cloth Dolls

Homemade primitives
Chase and other commercial
American rag child
Izannah Walker
American rag babies

Half Dolls

Wax Dolls

Poured wax
Wax coated

Paper Dolls

Uncut paper dolls

Collectible and Modern Dolls

Cloth

Käthe Kruse
Lenci
Chad Valley
Nora Welling

Celluloid

Composition

Hard Plastic

Vinyl

Advertising

Celebrity

Comic Strip

Paper mache 1830's doll preserved in her original costume. She has painted brush-stroked hair and brown glass eyes. Her hands are leather. She is 19" tall.

Queen Ann type doll. This one is on a wood spindle with no legs. Her arms are rolled pieces of cloth probably nailed to the wood body piece. Her eyes are shell or enamel. Her costume is in such good condition because she has resided under an oval globe for 100 years or more.

Left, 18" Simon and Halbig 151. All original blue ribbon girl, exhibited under "German children marked Simon and Halbig."

Setting Up Classes for Competition

The classes and all the detailed directions for the competition must be set up, printed and mailed months (six is best) before the show or convention. Every little detail must be spelled out. It is best that the potential competitor know how the dolls will be judged. The judging sheets for each doll category, along with how the points are divided up are found within this book.

Ordinarily there will be a class for German dolls, a class for French dolls and so on. But as more and more dolls are entered and certain classes are bulging with excellent dolls, it is wise to divide and subdivide these classes, so more people will have a chance at rosettes and trophies. One example is the German dolls. This could be divided into baby dolls, toddlers, children dolls with painted eyes, children dolls with glass eyes, dolls with molded hair, dolls over 18", and adult figured dolls. It is seldom that any show will need all these divisions, but one or two could be chosen if there should be more dolls than can be accommodated in the main class. Sometimes these classes can be subdivided even after the dolls are in.

In shows having competition for soft dolls, these are usually divided into dolls made from a pattern and original design dolls. Felt dolls are usually divided the same way. Wood dolls are usually put in a class by themselves, because the entries are usually few.

Automaton, The Bubble Blower. Bubble liquid is added to his pewter dish and he blows bubbles. A fun doll in great condition. He was a blue ribbon boy in 1965. New or reproduction automatons cannot copy the intricate movements of the antique ones.

Competition Extras

If a club can come up with something special to add to their competition classes, it may bring a sizable number of people to the show. These are people who would not normally come to a doll show. In several areas, there has been a class for the novice or for the very first doll. This brought in new people and encouraged their endeavors.

A group of 4-H boys and girls made dolls during the year. They were invited to enter their dolls in a special class for 4-H'ers with no entrance fee. There were 26 dolls entered. It was estimated that all 26 children, their friends, and many of their parents and relatives swelled the show.

Were there any dolls made by the senior citizens? Be sure the retirement apartments and homes know about the show. They often have doll classes in their recreation centers. Try to make arrangements for transportation for these groups.

Miniature organizations make dollhouses and dollhouse dolls that make great exhibits in classes by themselves.

There are special classes in smocking for doll clothes held in some doll classes. Have a class for these garments. Many classes are held in hat and bonnet making, which can be shown on unpainted shoulder heads or dolls.

In other words, make classes to fit special groups, or special doll related things. This will make your show a little different and increase attendance. Sometimes these special classes can increase the show's publicity.

Other clubs pick up the local history, area doings, holidays and national happenings. One example was the repairing of the Statue of Liberty. The theme was American dolls for the 4th of July, representing the American way of life. Any and all ideas could be worked in.

In Atlanta a special exhibit of Ella Smith dolls and black dolls were shown, because these dolls were made in that area. Almost every area has something unique, either in the past or present, that can go along with dolls. A New Jersey doll show put on a special exhibit or class for the Fulper dolls.

How about a Zane Grey Class of artist dolls? Or, is there an ethnic group that would like to show off their dolls or costumes?

Have you also considered having a video tape running in a corner of the exhibit hall? This spot with a few chairs makes a place for the tired. The tape could be exhibits from last year or antique dolls for inspirations.

Exhibit Classes for Seamstresses

We have come to the conclusion that dolls entered in competition, for the most part, should be dressed. These costumes play such an important part in the presentation of the doll, that it would be unfair not to recognize the workmanship and the skill of the doll world's fine couturiers. Therefore, appropriate classes should be set up for these designers and seamstresses. Depending on the number of entries expected, the show could include one or more of the following:

1. Costume for a French doll from the costumer's original pattern. Show original sketches and pattern pieces.
2. Doll costumed to look like a child in an antique photo. Show photo with doll.
3. French doll bonnets on appropriate head or doll.
4. Doll hat on appropriate head or doll.
5. Baby's christening outfit (2 pieces or more).
6. Crocheted costume for small doll.
7. Baby's knit outfit (2 or 3 piece).
8. German child doll outfit on appropriate doll, including smocking.
9. Costume for lady doll either French or German.

These costumes can be shown on reproduction or antique dolls. The dolls will only be judged in regards to their appropriateness to the costume.

In some contests, the costumer could be asked to display their costumes on dolls with unpainted faces, which would be easier for those who are not dollmakers. This is a matter of choice for the judging committees.

In small shows some of these classes can be combined into categories, such as crocheting and knitting, or hats and bonnets. New classes can be set up that will match the dolls entered in the reproduction classes. For instance, under German Children Dolls, a class might call for the doll to be dressed in a regional outfit. Here the dollmaker and the costumer could get together and make two dolls, each dressed the same. Then, one could be entered by the dollmaker and one by the costumer in their respective classes.

Classes for couturiers can change from year to year. With some research, you can find out what doll clubs have been making during the preceding year. Often times, there may have been some classes in hat or bonnet making or smocking, and they will probably love to show off their talents at the next show.

Left, 23" Bru Jne 8 with leather body and legs in excellent condition.

These are examples of competition regulations and categories to help you set up your own judging competition.

DEALERS FIRST CHOICE, INC.
Doll, Miniature & Toy Show
Las Vegas, Nevada

April 11-12, 1987
Hacienda Hotel Matador Arena
3950 S Las Vegas Blvd.

EXAMPLE ONLY

COMPETITION REGULATIONS

Mildred Seeley's Educational Judging System will be used in selecting dolls for awards and trophies entered in Dealers Choice Competitions. Each doll is judged on its own merits and given the award it deserves by certified, experienced judges.

Only accessories originally produced with the doll will be accepted with dolls entered in competition.

Commercial doll kits, dolls made with studio markings, or copies of dolls that may still be under copyright protection will not be allowed.

Owners names or initials on dolls must be covered with tape.

ALL dolls MUST be on a stand supplied by the exhibitor. Baby dolls that sit without additional assistance will be accepted; otherwise a stand must accompany the doll.

Insuring dolls will be the responsibility of the exhibitor.

Dealers First Choice, Inc. will have security guards on duty the night the dolls are registered until they are returned to the owners. During Doll Show & Sale days the exhibit dolls will be roped off for public viewing with adequate guards on duty.

Competitive Registration Entries must be postmarked by: April 1, 1987.

Dolls mailed in for exhibition registration will not be accepted. Entries will be accepted at the Hacienda Hotel Matador Arena Seville Rooms for registration on:

Thursday, April 9, 1987 10:00am - 8:00pm

Claim check (receipt) will be given to entrant at point of entry for articles entered.

Packing containers must be removed from Arena by owners immediately. Fire regulations prevent storage of these materials during exhibitions.

Dolls may be picked up by owners presenting a copy of their receipt on Sunday, April 12, 4:00pm - 8:00pm. Dolls cannot be removed prior to this time.

Dolls will be judged on Friday, April 10, 1987.

For information, contact:	Before March 23, 1987	After March 23, 1987
Louise Mulholland	12904 Holmes Pt. Dr. NE Kirkland, WA 98034 206-823-6197	3040 E Charleston #2021 Las Vegas, NV 89104 702-457-6199

EXAMPLE ONLY

DEALERS FIRST CHOICE, INC
Doll, Miniature & Toy Show

COMPETITION CATEGORIES

1. ANTIQUE
   a. Bisque
   b. Other (Wood, Wax, Rubber,Metal,etc)

2. ANTIQUE BABY DOLLS (bent legs)
   a. Bisque
   b. Composition
   c. Other

3. CHINA
   a. Fashion
   b. Half Dolls
   c. Other

4. COMPOSITION (except baby dolls)

5. CELLULOID

6. CLOTH
   a. Prior to 1950
   b. After 1950

7. ETHNIC
   a. Antique
   b. Modern
   c. Reproduction

8. MINIATURES (under 8")

9. PAIRS
   a. Before 1950
   b. After 1950

10. REPRODUCTION
   a. French
   b. German
   c. Other

11. TEDDY BEAR DOLLS
   a. 1851 - 1950
   b. 1950 - 1985

12. MODERN 1940 - 1950
   a. Hard Plastic
   b. Vinyl
   c. Other

13. ORIGINAL ARTIST
   a. Bisque
   b. Soft Sculpture
   c. Wooden
   d. Other

14. COSTUMED BY OWNERS
   a. Baby
   b. Fashion
   c. Historical
   d. Other

15. CLOWNS
   a. 1890 - 1930
   b. 1930 - 1950
   c. 1950 - 1985

16. POTPOURRI
   Any doll which does not fit any of the listed categories - or any doll which is the only doll entered in a category.

Exhibitor's # ____________ Class ________
Maker of doll ____________
Head markings ____________
Body markings ____________
Circa (approximate date) ____________
Repairs, damages ____________
Photo of antique doll in ____________ page ____
Comments: ____________

Other Doll Categories

3 x 5 card MUST accompany each doll, typed or printed by doll owner.

Exhibitor's # ____________
Class ____________
*Professional ____________
*Non-Professional ____________
*Senior ____________
*Novice ____________
*Other ____________
Head markings ____________
Mold Co. ____________
Circa of antique doll ____________
Photo of antique doll in ____________ page ____

Reproduction Doll Category

3 x 5 card MUST accompany each doll, typed or printed by doll owner.

MILDRED SEELEY'S EDJS EDUCATIONAL DOLL JUDGING SYSTEM

JUDGING EXERCISE

*These are German children dolls under 18". Want to judge them? Judging from a photo is like judging dolls to buy from an auction catalog—nearly impossible. (L-R) Doll 1 is a S&H 919; a rare doll but she has a small eye chip. Doll 2, marked Special, is too large for this class and must be disqualified. Doll 3 is an S&H without a number. It is in fine condition with a replaced wig, flirty eyes that work and all old clothing. Doll 4 is a completely original K*R 117N with flirty eyes that work. The shoes are off to show her perfect feet. Doll 5 is a common A.M. 390 with worn-looking original clothing. It has a replaced wig. Doll 6 is an A.M. 390 in a poor costume, has a replaced wig, and no underclothing or shoes.*

Stop: Judge these dolls yourself.

The in-training judges gave blue ribbons to Dolls 3 and 4, a red ribbon to Doll 1 and a white ribbon to Doll 5, and no award to Doll 6.

It is very difficult to judge these dolls without seeing them in person. You cannot read the exhibit cards, nor can you see eye chips, wear or broken fingers.

If I were judging, I would give the very rare S&H 119 (Doll 1) with all original clothing, wig and shoes, a blue ribbon. I feel the tiny eye chip is part of the "wear and tear" for a doll her age. I would give doll 4 a red ribbon, because she is a quite common doll. She is also a late doll made in the 20's. For the others, I would judge them the same way as the in-training judges did.

36" Jumeau marked Tête but with applied ears. Body, head and costume are in A-1 condition.

Special Awards and Publicity for the Winners

Awards for Teachers

We have many, many excellent teachers and seminar instructors throughout the world. It is seldom that these teachers get recognition for their fine instruction. Most of these teachers are so busy that they cannot enter dolls in competition themselves. Many are on the road or busy with classes of students working on competition projects.

We want to encourage these teachers to get their students to compete. Many teachers are just as happy or happier if their student wins an award, as they would be if they won it themselves (a trait of a true teacher).

So why not give an award to the teacher having the most student awards of red, or above? Give one point for a red; two for a blue; and five points for a rosette.

Teachers need recognition too, and this, in some small way, will call attention to the best teachers.

In Great Britain, blue is associated with royalty, thus the term royal blue.

Karen Milk's rosette winner.

I chose Patty Chaddock's A.T. for the professional trophy.

Publicity for the Winners

Some good publicity for the doll or the dollmaker is an additional part of winning. Actually, it is the publicity that comes with winning that may really do some good for the exhibitor.

A blue ribbon, a rosette or a trophy will pin the label "Excellent Dollmaker" on the winning dollmaker. This may in turn increase her doll sales or the number of students in her studio.

It is the competition manager's responsibility to get plenty of publicity for the show and the winners. It should be part of the competition's planning to arrange publicity for the competition winners. This will be publicity for the winners, but it will also be publicity for the current show and for future doll shows. In fact, most of it will be free publicity.

Dolls should be completely judged before the show's opening if possible. With conventions where people are bringing in dolls from long distances, this cannot be done. The next best thing is to have the judging done during the early show hours.

Getting publicity for the winners is hard work. But with some advanced planning, much of it can be done before the show starts.

Call local newspapers, local T.V. stations and educational cable channels. Give them the time that the judging will be completed. Try to arrange for a doll magazine to be represented at the show.

The most valuable suggestion I can give to those managing the winner's publicity is to write a press release complete with photos. Deliver or mail it to local papers that cannot attend. Also, mail it to doll magazines as a report.

Write one or two paragraphs about the doll show, include in the first paragraph the where and when; put on by whom; and add something concerning the size of the show and attendance. Have black and white glossies of the winners available for the papers and magazines, along with a list of the top winners. Red ribbon winners should be listed in the last paragraph. If there is sufficient room, the paper will print these too. A prepared press release will make the show information handy and easy for the newspapers to reproduce. It will also ensure that the correct information is reported, such as the name of the show with the winners' names spelled correctly with their appropriate awards. The extra work is worth it. This should be done and ready to distribute when judging is completed. The "one hour photo" developers are helpful here.

If you have reporters present, give them the press release and winners' list.

Dollmakers are like most other people, they love publicity. You will double the number of dolls exhibited at the next show, if the dollmakers receive really good publicity.

Once again, publicity for the dollmaker is good publicity for the show. Locally, it brings in a larger crowd of onlookers. It might also inspire

BIG
BABY

a few to start dollmaking. On a worldwide scale, the doll magazines will provide publicity for your show as well as the individual winners.

Publicity is free advertising, and it's just as important as paid advertising.

More Glory for the Competition Winners

Doll shows that run more than one day usually have some kind of get-together where the winners are presented with rosettes and trophies. Here the judges are introduced; the show's workers are thanked; and very special awards are given out. And if the show has a very special guest, he or she is honored here also.

The responsibility for organizing this get-together sometimes falls on the competition committee, the show chairman, or a special committee set up for this purpose. At the shows where I have been the guest of honor, many different types of things have been successful. At the Zion, Illinois show several years ago they put on a scrumptious banquet. Another year, they had a catered cocktail party. I have been to breakfasts or champagne breakfasts in Colorado and California. All these types of parties seem to be successful.

Some of these parties are completely sponsored by the doll show, while others must sell modest priced tickets to be able to afford the affair they desire.

Besides the awards and thank you's, often times there is a short doll program. Slide programs seem to be most popular.

As a source of income for these banquets, sometimes dolls are donated and auctioned off at the dinner.

All of these affairs give plenty of time for taking pictures of the award winners and their trophies.

Any one of these party-type functions seems to melt the ice and get doll collectors and dollmakers visiting together. It creates a warm feeling for the whole show, including workers, winners and participants.

In one instance, a fancy tea was held for the winners right in one corner of the exhibit room. This was a very lovely affair. Everyone could sip her tea, view the exhibit and photograph the winners.

In all of these party-like functions, with the exception of the night banquet, the participants will have to come straight from their tables in the sales room. The point should be made that they are welcome to come as they are.

At a recent one day show the award winners were gathered at one end of the exhibit room. The trophies and rosettes were handed to the winners so that their friends and family could get photos. A few words of praise were given to all the people who entered dolls.

None of these things are essential, but they do round out the whole affair.

Special trophies are awarded while friends and family take pictures.

Opposite page, 24" rare Jumeau Character marked 203. "So you got all the blue ribbons, it's obvious."

Educational Tours and Doll Shows

At some of the doll shows a new educational feature has been added. These are tours through the doll exhibits with a knowledgeable guide. A person who knows the dolls and the judging takes groups of people through the exhibit, explaining the judging and pointing out the special features of each doll. Sometimes the judge, judge's assistant, or judge-in-training act as guides. These guides must be very experienced in order to answer questions about the dolls. (Exhibitor cards will help here.)

These tours are very popular with people exhibiting their dolls. They get an inside view of what the judges thought and the "why's" of the judging. "Would-be" and "next-time" exhibitors find these tours tremendously helpful. Doll collectors and potential doll buyers are especially interested in these tours.

They can also be geared toward special groups, such as children's groups, the elderly, or special doll clubs.

The tours can be one of the most educational things at a doll show. Often, people sign up early for a tour and then return later for their tour. Half hour tours for a fairly large exhibit seem to be long enough. There shouldn't be more than ten people in a group so that all can see and hear. The white-gloved guide is allowed to pick up the dolls for better showing. At very large shows the tours are broken down to cover only one section of dolls, preferably the guides will cover the dolls they know best. This way the public can choose to go through only those parts of the exhibit that they are interested in.

These mini doll tours encourage more people to exhibit their dolls. They also reach people outside of the doll clubs. They are an educational value equal to the exhibit itself.

Right, 18" marked Huret. People will learn more about rare dolls like these after tours with good guides.

First of all consider the size of your house or apartment. If your house is huge, tiny dolls may look lost unless they are massed or grouped. Large dolls in a large house fit better. In a small apartment tiny or small dolls are a joy to arrange. Perhaps one large doll can be carefully placed in an apartment.

The next consideration is the display space or your cabinet size. Most of us have doll cabinets. Some of these have adjustable shelves to accommodate a range of sizes. I especially like globes to display individual dolls on side tables, coffee tables, and even pillars like a sculpture. The size of each doll must be taken into consideration so it fits both the pillar and display case.

As I have said before, dolls in boxes under the bed are not much fun, so collect dolls that you can display and enjoy each day. Exchange the others by sending them to auction.

Another consideration while judging for the right size is the doll's costuming. For the larger doll more yards of silk will be necessary, which can be expensive. Small pieces of antique lace are more available than larger pieces. If the doll is sent out to be costumed, the couturier charges by the size of the doll.

In judging dolls to buy, think what you are going to do with the doll. Are you an exhibitor at shows or conventions? If so, medium or small sizes are easier to carry, to fly with, and to manage for exhibiting.

Many antique dolls are not purchased perfect and will need repairs. Here again, small or medium sized dolls are less expensive. For example, an eye replacement for small eyes costs very little; but when you get into the very large eyes, they will cost as much as $80.00 per pair. Other repairs or replaced parts are also more expensive on the larger dolls.

In the last year or so there has been a change in doll prices that should be noted by the collector. Formerly, the larger the doll; the higher the price. Not so anymore. Some of the tiny dolls are selling for higher prices than the larger dolls. These dolls are the well-decorated, older dolls of Steiner, Jumeau, Bru, Kestner, S & H and other reputable dollmakers. Small dolls with poor bisque, poor painting and poor costumes are still of little value.

So while judging dolls to add to your collection, consider the size very carefully. This also applies when purchasing reproduction dolls or even if you are making your own dolls. The size of the doll is very important!

Black French Fashion doll is 16" tall. Note the two rows of teeth and black eyes. Good cabinet-sized doll. She wears her original gold silk taffeta dress. She is on a leather body. This black doll is not found often, and her rarity alone will gain her points over the other fashions.

The Shape

The shape of a doll is most important to a collector. There are just three main shapes to consider: the realistically proportioned adult doll, the chubby bent limbed baby doll, and the child doll. The adult figure doll could be French Fashion dolls, men dolls, German lady dolls (like the Gibson Girls) or modern lady dolls. The baby dolls could be cloth bodied babies, composition or plastic bodied dolls—anything representing a child under 2. The children dolls are the most popular and encompass by

Opposite page, 36" Bru Jne 15. Not everyone would want a big Bru like this one. Big dolls are hard for older people to handle.

Before 1897, baby dolls had the same shape as other dolls—straight legs and arms. The only difference was that they were dressed as babies. Today, you rarely find one of these dolls. This 15" Steiner Series "C" with wire eyes is in mint condition. She is completely original. A superior doll and a blue ribbon personified.

far the largest group of dolls. These could be antique French children, German characters, googlies, dolly-faced dolls or the multitude of child-like dolls on the market today. These three shapes are the common shape of antique, reproduction and modern dolls on the collectors market.

Beginning collectors usually collect one of each shape and type while the advanced collector knows where her real interest lies and specializes in the group of dolls that give her the greatest joy.

A doll collection can be any group of dolls. But a specialized collection usually takes into consideration the shape of the doll *first*. (I would like to add that a *specialized collection* where the doll is judged for *shape* is more fun. The hunt and the chase for these special dolls is invigorating, and the resulting collection is usually a fine investment.)

If the main doll shape in your collection is the five piece fat baby doll, then you must have plenty of room to display the dolls. Babies are usually best displayed in carriages, high chairs, rocking chairs and the like. A baby doll's legs do not fit well into crowded cabinets. So judge the shape and where you can display the doll before you buy.

The shape of the feminine figured lady doll is easy to display. She will stand many deep in a cabinet for protection. She looks beautiful under a dome or in a glass display case. She looks fine on a pillar. The lady doll when arranged with a piece of appropriate furniture, other lady dolls, or a tiny child doll, makes a great set-up or home-like arrangement. A few dolls can look like an expensive collection.

The shape of the child doll makes collecting, storing and displaying large numbers rather easy. They can be arranged with furniture, displayed in groups, or properly displayed alone.

It might be wise to mention the shape of automata, because these must have special consideration when added to your collection. Think of automata as box-like shapes. They need space all around them. Automata do not lend themselves to cabinets, being lined up, or put into groups. They need to be displayed alone where they can be easily wound for pure enjoyment. Their shape should be considered before they are purchased.

The shape of the doll makes a big difference for your collection. Child doll, fashion doll or baby: How will you display them? (L-R) 18"Eden Be'be', Averill Baby and Rohmer Fashion do not exhibit well together.

Your Skills

Judging dolls for your own collection is such a personal thing—each and every one of us has to decide just what we want, which ones we can afford, and what we will enjoy most.

There are those collectors who should and do consider their creativeness and skills when judging dolls for their collections. They judge the doll on the sales table or from the auction catalog quite differently from the general run of collectors. For instance, I have a friend who costumes dolls. She has a talent for putting together the right materials, the right colors, the right style of hat and dress for any doll. She and people like her would be financially wise and happier if they select dolls with no clothes or makeshift clothes. She is going to redress the doll anyway.

17" blue ribbon winning Heubachs. Dolls in the shape of children are my favorite, whether French or German.

25" doll marked P G for Pintel and Godchaux. Use your own skills to repair your dolls. Her wig was gone so I made her a mohair skin wig.

The gentleman collector who has a knack for refinishing bodies should judge dolls with his skill in mind. He may even select a doll on the wrong body because he has spare bodies. If fixing bodies are his skill, then he judges doll bodies differently than ordinary collectors.

If you like to repair porcelain, you may want to buy a cracked or broken doll. Judge the doll by what you can do to the doll.

Some collectors are great at repairing sleep eyes or set eyes, some are good at making becoming wigs. So if the eyes or wig are the only problems, and you are a "fixer;" select the dolls that are in need.

In each instance the collector must judge the doll with her own repair skills in mind. Study the doll and judge if you can do it. Do not listen to dealers or friends. Many of the greatest dolls need help. Buying dolls this way is a savings, but it also gives the repairer a great feeling of accomplishment.

The same kind of thing holds true with collectors of Lenci dolls or even wood dolls. Judge the dolls with your own repair skills in mind.

Investment Dolls

There are dolls you might collect for investment and they will require another set of judging considerations. These dolls must be carefully studied along with the doll market. They can be used for making a profit in the same manner as gold coins or stocks and bonds. The wonderful thing about dolls for investment is that you can enjoy their loveliness all the while you have them. It is not like valuables locked in a safe deposit box. The dolls are a joy and can bring you happiness every time you pass them.

I have dolls that I call my investment dolls. They really fit into all the other judging categories for my collection too. For my investments I select dolls in the very expensive class. I pick dolls with universal appeal or beauty, well marked, excellent workmanship and condition, rarity and well dressed. By *universal appeal,* I mean dolls that are liked by most people instantly. Dolls with universal appeal are dolls that sell quickly and easily. A *well marked* doll is one with a known "birthmark" incised on her neck and hopefully a stamp mark on her body. By *workmanship*, I refer to the original creation of the doll, including the fine bisque, superior painting, good eyes, wonderful modeling, correct body proportions, good body shape and strong material. The *condition* of the doll is how the doll has stood up under the test of time and play. Condition takes into consideration the hairline cracks, chips, flakes, worn or replaced parts, missing or repaired fingers, the replaced wig, the new costume, or any other damage that has happened to the doll over the last hundred or so years.

Rarity of the doll is very important when considering investment dolls. If thousands of this particular doll were made, then the doll will never be a great investment doll. The fewer the dolls, the greater the chance for profit when the doll is sold.

24'' doll marked 5-H. Her maker was recently researched to be Halopeau, successor to Barrois. This doll is one of the finest investments we made.

13'' Andre Jean Thuillier. If they were giving blue ribbons for universal appeal, this A.T. would have one.

A costume which is preferably original and one you can preserve will be a great asset in an investment doll. Collectors will always pay more for a doll in original costume.

The age of the doll must be taken into consideration. But older dolls are not always more valuable. For instance, many china dolls are older than the Marque dolls; yet, you cannot compare for investment.

Money invested in expensive dolls is no instant winner. You cannot buy a high priced doll today and expect to sell it for a huge profit tomorrow—although some dealers do. Generally, elapsed time is what raises the price of dolls. Look at the current price of A.T.'s from $12,000 in 1986 to $68,000 in 1989. Over the forty to fifty years that I have collected, the price of top dolls has always gone up. Of course, there may come a time!

Recently I have seen wonderful evidence of the security built into a doll collection. One well known collector/writer sold the remainder of her doll collection for somewhat over three-quarters of a million dollars. These are dolls that were bought 30 years ago for less than one-tenth of their present-day selling prices. In another instance, a smaller all French collection gathered in the 1940s sold for about $900,000. Every day I am aware of dolls being sold for twice to twenty times the price the owner paid 10 to 30 years ago. I know, I have done it myself many times over.

While buying dolls for investment, I say again, study the market. Dolls that come up at every auction and every sales room many times a year are not investment dolls. These dolls are not rare enough.

Dolls that are cracked or broken and repaired are not investment dolls, although sometimes this is not true. I used to think investment dolls needed to be absolutely perfect, but they don't.

Some of the rarer dolls that make good investment dolls *when* they have all the other qualifications are:

- Hurets
- Pans
- Mothereaux
- H-Dolls
- A.T.'s
- portrait Jumeaux
- Jumeau character dolls
- early Bru's
- some Schmitts
- rare K*R's
- SIE Steiners
- some beautiful unmarked or unknown dolls
- some character dolls
- perhaps Pintel & Godchaux
- Mascotte
- articulated wood bodied French Fashions
- some marked Hurets or Rohmer chinas
- working mechanicals
- There are others also.

I find that in order to get one of these fabulous dolls with all the necessary qualifications, I must pay a higher price or what I consider an outrageous price to get the doll. Then I have to wait for a year or so for the price at auction to even catch up. So far it always has. For example, I paid $45,000 for a Pan doll from a Florida museum. At the time, it looked as though I had made a mistake, but within eight months Theriault's auction sold one by the same maker, Henri Delcroix, for $47,000.

I collect dolls as fine art—something to enjoy and make daily life more like a continual sunrise.

The Doll's Appeal

I believe the most important judgment anyone can make in considering a doll is the doll's appeal. You often hear comments like, "The doll speaks to me." To build a collection that will give you long-term satisfaction and daily enjoyment, each doll you add must be one that appeals to *you*, not your club, your friend or the world, but to *you*. This personal appeal is so important! In fact, I think it is the most important judgment anyone should make while selecting a doll.

Size, shape, condition and investment are important considerations. But if the doll is one you cannot live without, do not pass her by. Forget all that I have told you to consider because the most important thing in doll collecting is happiness and pleasure. A doll that will always be "love at first sight" is the one you want.

Judging Family Dolls

If you are the fortunate person who has a family doll or several family dolls, *don't* think of judging them. Just accept these treasures and love them for their sentimental value. If you have your own old doll, your mother's doll or any doll that has come down from a relative or a friend, keep the doll and display it proudly. It is a part of your history. It is more valuable to you than to anyone anywhere. It may not be a Jumeau or a Bru but it is worth more sentimental value than any doll you can buy. My play dolls and my mother's doll were the nucleous of my collection, and they still hold prominent places in my cases.

Left, my famous Albert Marque dolls made in 1913, 22". These dolls have increased in value enormously since I first researched them. They are one of the best investment dolls.

Two of my play dolls and my mother's doll. (L-R) Armand Marseille, my mother's unmarked doll and a Heubach Koppelsdorf.

16" Bru Jne 5. Many people find Brus the most appealing doll.

22" A.T. by Thuillier. The perfect doll to choose for a reproduction mold, because she has universal appeal and is very rare. One like her sold for $67,000 in 1989.

MILDRED SEELEY'S EDJS EDUCATIONAL DOLL JUDGING SYSTEM

JUDGING EXERCISE

Four F.G.s 17" to 21". Which would you choose for your collection? Which would you choose to exhibit to win a blue ribbon? Would one be a better investment than the others?

(L-R) Doll 1 in aqua silk and antique lace is marked F.C.G.; Doll 2 in plaid silk taffeta is marked F. 2/O.G.; Doll 3 in lace is marked F.8.G.; Doll 4 in cream silk and antique lace is marked F.G. in a scroll.

All the dolls have been redressed at some point. All wear good antique shoes. All the bisque and bodies are in excellent condition without chips or cracks. The wigs on Dolls 3 and 4 have been replaced with human hair. Dolls 1 and 2 have mohair wigs.

Stop: Judge these dolls yourself.

Now make your choices for your collection, blue ribbon winners or investment purposes.

In my cabinet, fat little Doll 3 always appeals to onlookers. She is a good old doll and the shape of her face makes her interesting. I chose her to add to my collection.

Expecting to win a blue ribbon, I would exhibit Doll 2. She has a leather body and bisque hands. She is much older than all the other dolls. She is not the typical F.G.

Dolls 1, 2 and 3 are the best investment dolls. They are better than Doll 4 because they are rarer and older.

These dolls are all fine quality and could be considered good collector's dolls.

MILDRED SEELEY'S EDJS EDUCATIONAL DOLL JUDGING SYSTEM

JUDGING EXERCISE

Which of these Jumeaux would you choose for your collection if you could have just one? All are the same price and about the same size. (L-R) Dolls 1-3 are marked Tête Dépose Jumeau. Doll 4 is marked BL and Doll 5 is marked Paris Be'be'.

Stop: Judge these dolls yourself.

In the photo Doll 2 is certainly the cutest and has the most appeal. Dolls 1, 2 and 3 are all the same mold face. The wigs on Dolls 2,3 and 5 are mohair; Dolls 1 and 4 have human hair. All five wear original costumes and shoes.

If you choose Doll 2—she is in her commercial chemise and she has good Jumeau socks and shoes. Her hair has not been touched and she is in her original box and in unplayed-with condition. She is an excellent choice.

If you choose Doll 4—she is the rarest of the dolls, having been made by Jumeau for the Louvre Store. Be'be''s Louvre she is called. I believe her wig has been replaced. Her costume shows some fading and deterioration. She is earlier than Doll 2.

My choice would be Doll 3. She is perfect and all original. She is the oldest of the Jumeaux in this line-up.

All of these Jumeaux are blue ribbon quality, so any one that you choose would be a good buy.

22" doll marked J.M. The maker is still unknown. Her strange body would probably keep her from winning a blue ribbon.

Judging Dolls for Yourself and Others

Judging Unmarked and Unknown Dolls

There are thousands of unmarked dolls in many categories. Most of these dolls are easily identified by their material and by their structure. This especially applies to dolls made after 1920. People still remember when the doll came out or that they played with that type of doll.

The really lost "kids" or the "orphans" are those bisque headed dolls made before 1900 with no identification letters or numbers on the back of their heads. These dolls are often listed in doll auction catalogs as "mystery" dolls. These are the dolls that go to competition and find no place to stand. They are outcasts that do not fit into any category.

The numbers, initials, letters and names on the back of the dolls' heads act like their birth certificates. They remain with the doll as identification for as long as the doll lasts. Other lost "kids" are ones marked with letters or markings that cannot be identified.

More and more research is being done, and each year a few more of these come to light. There are both French and German dolls that fall into this "mystery" class. Sometimes we are not even certain about their country or origin. Most of these dolls are very early dolls. They were made before dollmaking competition became so keen. At that time, marking and registration were not considered necessary.

Kiss throwing late Jumeau in an all original costume.

I have a somewhat different attitude about these unknown dolls. I believe at least one unknown doll is great in every collection. But I don't want just any unmarked doll or one with unknown markings. These should be judged like other dolls. You still must consider appeal or beauty, construction and painting, condition and rarity (is assumed if it is unknown). I put my money on beauty and appeal.

Sometime ago I was brought a doll marked JJ. There were several theories about the maker of this doll. I had never examined one before. The antique costume was spectacular, and the doll's condition was excellent. Her eyes were lovely, but the painting was a poor quality. The nose dots were so low she looked like she had a bloody nose. The lip paint was somewhat crude with orange-red paint. I felt the doll did not reflect the quality I wanted in my collection. Although she was rare, I did not buy her. I mentally date the doll by the color of her china paint as 1898 or later.

A couple of years ago a dealer had a really old doll marked J.M. It was the kind of doll I just love. She had a charming child-like face. Her mark is still unknown, although some have suggested that J.M. stood for J. Mattias who worked with Steiner. But all the telltale signs seem to date the doll much older. For example, the deep mauve blush over her eyes was not being used at that date.

Another "mystery" doll that I have is one marked with red china paint H l. It is not one of the incised H-Dolls, but one whose painting is not like any in my collection. Another in my collection is a wonderful French baby doll that has a)(on her head. A sister doll has nothing but O. These are very old dolls with skin wigs and original clothing over their well-shaped paper mache bodies.

Right, early French doll marked only with a)(. is a wonderful blue ribbon attraction for any collection.

There are many so-called Belton dolls circulating with no markings and closed heads. Some of these may be French, but most are German. Each of these must also be judged for their own merits.

Up until recently, the wonderful H-Dolls had no known maker. No H-Doll had ever come up at auction until Theriaults sold one of mine in January 1990. At the time their research in France revealed that Halopeau made these dolls between 1882-1888. The doll was sold for $100,000, a record for bisque dolls, or any doll in this country. The H-Doll's beauty, construction, fine painting, and rarity dictate their desirability and price. There are few dolls that rate with the H-Dolls. This doll was both a joy for me to own and an excellent investment.

Is It French or German?

Along the way we all have to make a judgment regarding whether an unmarked or unknown doll is French or German. There are some things we can look for that may indicate a French doll. There are other things that are *usually so* and still others that are so on the older French dolls. Many times we say, "French dolls have..." only to find there is an exception in the next collection we view. To make it still more difficult, some of the late French dolls were made in Germany. Be slow to make a judgment, check out everything.

Usually you can look at a doll and say with confidence, "In my opinion this doll is French or German." Most dolls have that certain French or German look.

The following are the characteristics I look for in a French doll:

*1. Sliced off head—the bisque is cut off at the top on a decided slant.
Exception: Belton heads or closed heads.

*2. Paperweight eyes—the very deep rounded out eyes (not sleep eyes).
Exception 1: Some of the late French dolls had sleep eyes.
Exception 2: Some had Steiner wire eyes.
Exception 3: Some early German dolls had set eyes.

*3. Absence of rim at the top of the head—most French dolls have no rim, just the thickness of the bisque. German dolls have a rim to prevent warping during firing.
Exception: French dolls made in Germany and some late French heads.

*4. Applied ears—ears that have been added to the greenware, found on many French heads made before 1890.

Right, upon close inspection this J.M. passes all the tests for a French doll.

*5. Pressed bisque heads—heads that were made by pressing slabs of moist clay into mold pieces. Inside of the head is rough; nose and lips solid or opaque when held to the light.
6. Pierced ears—pierced through the lobe or into the head.
Exception: A few older German dolls had pierced ears.
*7. Closed mouth—most of the French dolls had closed mouths.
Exception: Some Steiners, some F.G.'s, and some late Jumeaux had open mouths. Some very old German dolls, such as Kestner, had closed mouths.
*8. Cork pate—Only the French used cork pates.
Exception 1: Steiner used purple cardboard.
Exception 2: Pates can be changed from doll to doll.
9. Pale bisque—usually the bisque color is a lighter shade for French dolls than for German dolls.
Exceptions: There are plenty.
*10. Mauve eye shadow—this color was used over the eyes only on the very old French dolls.
11. Feathered brows—French dolls have feathered brows.
Exception: Sometimes German dolls have feathered brows.
12. Lips—accent line on lips of French dolls are more or less alike, while many German dolls have no accent line or a different type.
Exception: Many very late French dolls had no accent lines.
13. Straight wrist—many of the early French bodies had straight wrists, later ones had jointed wrists.
Exception: One of the most used German Kestner bodies also had straight wrists.
14. French clothing—factory-made chemises and couturier designed costumes for French dolls can usually be identified.
Exception: Clothing can be changed from doll to doll or have no clothes.

In my opinion, the items marked with an * are the most reliable.

Is It Antique or Reproduction?

Sometimes I am asked to judge a doll that I would rather not judge. None of us wants to play God. Sometimes I may wiggle and squirm, but finally I am forced to face what must be done in fairness to the doll world and the collector at hand.

Recently, one of these bad times came up. I had to face the bad news about a doll, then tell the doll dealer so she could tell the collector, who

Right, marked only 4-H. The best way to protect yourself from buying a reproduction instead of an antique is to study the old dolls and photos.

then spread the bad news to the auction house, and on down the chain, *all bad news.*

This is what happened. A very reputable doll dealer called me for my opinion. She had a darling little black Bru in her hands that she was considering buying for resale. The price was around $18,000. She described the doll over the phone: old black hair, old cork pate, old split cotton drawers, maroon satin dress, perfect shining brown leather body and perfect bisque hands. (I noted to myself, that although the body and hands are perfect, they could be old.) I kept asking her, "How is the doll marked and what is on her shoulder plate?" She answered, "I can't find anything except Bru Jne; there are no numbers anywhere. There are no markings on the shoulder plate at all."

We discussed this scary lack of numbers, and we found it very disturbing. She decided to send me the doll "overnight" mail, and I was to send it back the same way. The doll was shipped all the way from the East Coast to my home in Arizona for examination.

I always hate to do this because I'm afraid of what I might find. Now that Brus and other good French dolls are selling anywhere from $24,000 to $60,000, someone will want to turn his or her reproduction talents into high profits. The dishonest and greedy are always with us. We are thankful the doll world has so few of them.

The doll arrived. I lifted her from the box and my first reaction was—what a darling doll! But after a closer look and some study, I stated the doll is a reproduction. All of my antique Brus have numbers on the head and on the shoulder plate, and this doll's number has been removed. The numbers would have indicated the doll's actual size. A reproduction would be a size smaller than this number would indicate.

The eyes are new and so is the plaster they are set with. There is no marking or indication that they have been reset or replaced.

The inside of the head shows a rim around the top which my old Brus don't have. Antique Bru heads before 1890 were made by pressing porcelain clay slabs into the mold parts. These heads have no top rim, unlike heads that were made from poured clay (slip). These early heads were cut on a slant with only the thickness of the clay forming the top edge of the head.

Inside the head new shiny hardware fastens the head to the body. In order to refasten an old head to a body with new hardware, the leather strips around the shoulder plate must be removed. These are difficult to remove, and they do not come off easily in one piece. You will inevitably tear them in some places. These strips have never been removed, because they are not torn.

The painting does not match the antique's either. The basic brown is a nice color. I even like it better than the color of my old black Bru. But this doll had blushed cheeks over the brown. I have never seen an antique black or brown doll with *any* blushing over the cheeks. The brows were perfectly matched with black matte. The black Brus that I have seen, and

Small black Bru Jne from another auction house. The doll has NO number.

This is the antique Black Bru's rim.

the one that I own have mismatched eyebrows like all Brus. Also the brows on my black Bru and all the others that I have seen were painted with a bit of gloss mixed in with the black. This Bru's brows are dead matte. Also on the old dolls, the lashes always have blunt-ended strokes on one eye and pointed strokes on the other. This doll's lashes did not. The mouth was not the right color and the lips were not painted in between like my old doll's lips. Because I have studied the painting on the antique dolls so much and so often, all the little differences on this doll stick out. Again, *in my opinion* this doll looks very much as though it had come from one of the molds we produced fifteen years ago, including the hands.

The leather body was exceptionally well done. It looked as though it had been dyed and polished in a shoe repair shop. The body was an exact copy of our Bru Jne 6 "Comfort." Three years ago I made a copy of Comfort's very intricate body. I know that the pattern went many places around the world. In addition, the pinking on Bru bodies was not done with pinking shears or modern equipment, but with a metal die, a stamping device. It is obvious the body maker had problems trying to imitate the old methods.

The doll's plump leather body with leather feet and sewn-in toes was used on the very early Brus before 1890.

As I studied this little Bru, a picture from an auction book flashed into my mind. I went immediately to check the book. At Frasher's Auction on July 19, 1989, number 54 was a small black Bru marked Bru Jne with no numbers. There was a picture and it looked so much like the little Bru that I held in my hands, that I thought it was the same doll. The painting and the eyes were identical. It had to be a sister doll done by the same person. The auction people were wary about the doll, because they would not guarantee its authenticity. Even so, the doll sold for $2,500 which is a high price for a copy, but still a far cry from the $18,000 that the dealer was about to pay for this doll.

You may have to judge whether a doll is a reproduction or an antique, perhaps even one that you intend to buy for your collection. Reproduction dolls are so good now, that you may have to turn into a detective. Use the same type of criteria I used to determine whether it is an antique or a reproduction.

The best way to tell a reproduction from an antique is to compare the questionable doll with a known antique whenever possible. The Bru on the left is from my collection.

The Story Behind the Doll—Is It Important?

How important is the story behind the doll? Is it important to know who owned the doll or where the doll has been? Will you judge a doll differently if you know her provenance? Will you pay more for a doll with a known background?

Dolls with provenance are great for museums, because their stories can be printed and exhibited along with the dolls to create greater interest. It is also the museum's duty to preserve the doll's history.

I believe doll dealers just hate to bother with the story connected to a doll. Even names, dates and labels are often lost.

Black Bru sold at auction. Photo courtesy of Frasher's Auctions.

FIRST PRIZE
UNITED
FEDERATION
DOLL CLUBS
ANNUAL
EXHIBITION

In home collections some people think stories about their dolls are great, while others could care less. As for me, I love to know just where the doll has come from and when. Here is an example of my search for the provenance of a recently purchased pair of dolls:

It was about fifteen years ago when I was traveling down through the Smoky Mountains and met a lady with a nice collection of dolls. In the collection I saw a pair of rather regal-looking wood dolls standing among fine French bisque dolls. With Jumeaux and Brus nearby I hardly noticed the pair. The owner and I became good friends and over the fifteen years since I met her, she kept calling my attention to that wooden pair of dolls. I had little interest in them, especially since she knew nothing about who made them, or where they were made. No, I didn't want to buy them.

Recently, the lady and I had another go-around about the wood dolls. They were the only dolls in her collection, since the others had been sold. She said the dolls had been exhibited at the UFDC in 1966 in Chicago where they took a blue ribbon. Still, no one identified them. A well known collector knew they were portraits of royalty but she wasn't sure of whom.

Before buying, we had the following discussion:

"Are the dolls marked?" She replied, "I have never undressed the dolls, because this would damage their wonderful costumes. There are no marks that I can see."

I asked, "Where did you get the dolls?"

"Harriet Miller of Arlington, Vermont, an antique dealer. Mr. Miller had a government job and worked a portion of each year in Paris. She brought many of the dolls in my collection back from Paris. She brought this pair back in 1940."

"Would you remember how much you paid for them?" I asked.

"I never paid over $300 for any doll, because that was my limit. I am sure I paid less than $300 for the pair."

These dolls had been in the same place for nearly fifty years. I had seen them briefly just once in the fifteen years I had known about them. I still wasn't convinced that I wanted them.

"Why do you want such a high price for them?" I asked her.

She replied, "I am sure they are rare dolls, because no one can identify them. And I haven't seen any like them during my fifty years of doll collecting."

Opposite page, 22" Josef Kubelka dolls. The lady doll has a recessed scalp with inset hair. These Kubelka wood dolls may be the only ones in existence. They were made about 1887.

We finally agreed that I would buy them at a little less than her price and a lot more than mine. All of this took place between my dear friend, the doll collector, and me over the telephone. I sent the check. I am sure the dolls arrived before the check.

I opened the box filled with foam peanuts and I pulled out the lady doll. Before I had even unwrapped her completely, I knew what she was. I remembered a page in a doll magazine featuring these beautiful dolls by Josef Kubelka. I had never seen one before, yet I felt positive in my identification. Why hadn't I identified the dolls earlier? It had been fifteen years since I had seen them, and they were behind glass and not well lighted. Also, my interest was mainly in French bisque and I didn't pay much attention to them.

This pair of dolls, a man and woman, are 22" tall. They are on rather rough jointed bodies. They are well-balanced, well-proportioned, beautifully painted dolls. Their head and hands are also wood. Their glass eyes (the man's are dark brown, the lady's are hazel) are not the usual glass eyes used in dolls.

Both the lady and the man have striking adult features different from any doll I know. Their modeling is realistic, and their general expression is one of regal solemnity tinged with sadness. The lady is very captivating, very feminine. The great detail in their painting gives the impression that these dolls were not a production, nor were they made in any large numbers. Although my dolls are wood and not porcelain, their unusual facial descriptions match the facial descriptions used for the bisque Kubelka in the magazine article as well.

Their costumes are in excellent condition. The man has molded and painted hair, but the lady has the recessed scalp and inset hair which was probably the Kubelka patent of 1887. This lady doll has something the other three known Kubelka dolls do not have: extra painted curls and shading around the edges of the recessed hair.

According to researcher Florence Poisson, these dolls are considered French dolls even though Josef Kubelka was a Vienna dollmaker.

For me, a doll's story *does* make a difference. My Kubelka dolls are truly blue ribbon dolls, once they were researched and identified.

Another example is our A.T. Silver. She has a wonderful doll story for my collection.

The Tabor residence was the most pretentious on Capitol Hill in Denver. It was on Thirteenth Avenue and its grounds ran through Sherman to Grant Avenues. A brown stone wall ran around the lower end of the velvety lawn where the grounds sloped to two driveways leading to the stables. Tabor engaged five gardeners and housemen, two coachmen and two footmen. He had three carriages and six horses.

Two pairs of horses were jet black. One carriage was brown trimmed in red, another dark blue trimmed in gold. The inside was upholstered in

Right, 14" A.T. Silver from the estate of Baby Doe Tabor's daughter.

light blue satin. Another carriage was black trimmed in white with white satin upholstery. The horses had brass ornamented harnesses. Mrs. Tabor (Baby Doe) would order the carriage and horses that best suited the costume she was wearing that day.

On July 13, 1884, Elizabeth Bonduel Lillie Tabor was born. Her christening dress was hand-embroidered lace with diamond and gold pins and a tiny necklace with a diamond studded locket. That outfit supposedly cost $15,000.

This was just the place where one would expect to find a child holding a fine French doll. Lillie often cuddled her small but beautiful A.T. doll—nothing but the finest would do.

Many doll collectors are familiar with the story of Baby Doe and Horace Tabor and the silver mines of Leadville, Colorado.

This little A3T and a few old books were Lillie's only remaining belongings. She was living with the McCourt family, her grandparents, when she died. Baby Doe's nephew sold the doll and the books after the McCourts died.

Today, the doll is in fine condition. The head, shoulder plate and bisque hands are on a kid body. The doll was completely without clothing. This redressed doll now stands proudly in my showcase with her other A.T. friends.

Then, there is the story of "Comfort" and the many projects she worked for me.

Forty or fifty years ago around Albany, New York, on the poorer side of town, a lady lived who was seen for years going through the garbage and throw-outs of the city's well-to-do. Her bent figure, black coat and gray hair was a familiar sight. She always carried a battered shopping bag from one of Albany's finest stores.

When she died, the police found out that she had lived in a single basement room. Upon entering her room, they found it completely filled with dolls of all kinds, shapes and sizes.

The room had to be cleaned out. So they threw the dolls into large bags and delivered them to Lillian Sproul, who had a doll museum called "Yesteryears." She did not want to trouble with the dolls, because her husband was very sick. But the dolls were put in her garage anyway.

Lillian decided the dolls must be checked over before sending the lot off to the city dump. She took an hour or so each day to sort the dolls while she looked after her husband. She was on the very last bag of dolls when to her great surprise, she pulled out a blue-eyed Bru—a Bru, a marked Bru! She couldn't believe her eyes and took the doll in to show her husband. She put the doll on a dresser. "That doll will be some comfort to you for all of your work," he said. Lillian named the doll "Comfort," and the doll gave her enjoyment every time she looked at it.

Opposite page, Bru Comfort, marked Bru Jne 6 is 17". She has a plump leather body, leather feet and bisque hands.

Lillian made Comfort's costume using material from a very lovely old French silk gown. She copied the costume from a photo of another Bru. The underclothing looks all original. The shoes are marked, and the wig is original. Comfort was sold to me after Lillian's doll museum closed. I am sure the price she received for the Bru was a comfort.

I used Comfort as a porcelain plate design on my first plate in "The Doll Collection." The plate originally sold for $39.00. The edition sold out quickly and now the plate is being sold on the secondary market for $250.00. This has been a "comfort" to many plate collectors, especially those who bought two.

I used Comfort as a cover for my book, *Dollmaker's Workbook French Children Dolls*, and that book cover is one of my favorites. Comfort is now world-known.

Comfort stands with the other Bru dolls in my doll cabinet. Her appealing blue eyes charm all doll collectors. I cannot pass her without feeling good about possessing her.

Comfort has lived up to her name from the time she belonged to some little rich girl in Albany, through her years with the street lady, during her museum time, and now after being shared with the world.

Not all doll stories are happy, even if the doll is a Bru.

I was called to Bainbridge, New York, to look at a doll that Adeline Jones wanted to sell. With shaking hands the lady passed me the doll. It was a small Bru dressed in cranberry red. I checked the doll for cracks and offered her the going retail price for Brus. The woman was astounded that it was worth so much. Then she told me she was 89 and had kept the doll in her dresser drawer ever since she was married. She went on to tell me, "I didn't like the doll much because my grandmother had given it to me so I would stop sucking my thumb. I didn't stop, so I never really got to enjoy the doll until I was too big for dolls."

I think of Adeline whenever I pass the little Bru standing in my collection.

Another short story is Jennie's, the original owner of my incised Jumeau.

Jennie Mabel Hastings received this incised Jumeau doll when she was 6. The Hastings family lived in the mountainous area of Bovina, New York. Her father, Thomas E. Hastings, purchased the doll in 1886. He had a friend bring the doll from New York City. Jennie's mother had recently died and her father hoped the doll would help. It did. It became her constant companion. Today, the doll shows signs of tender love. Jennie gave me the doll in 1959.

This doll is dressed in a reproduction dress, but she still has her original beads, wig, and shoes. I call her Jennie.

Right, this Pan is a wonderful doll to reproduce because chances of owning one are extremely rare.

A jewel amongst jewels is Bru Jne 4, 16".

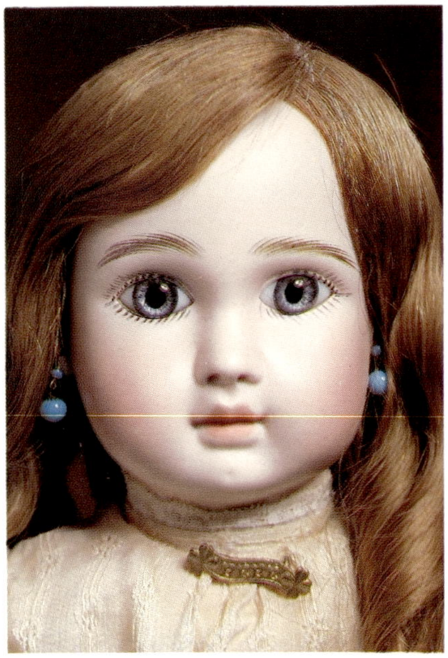

24" Steiner A would make a fine reproduction.

Dolls like these reproductions by Edna Miller (above) and Linda Cheek (below) will stand the test of time.

Provenance is where the doll came from and who has loved her. It might be considered just a "fun" thing to know, but it adds something special to my doll collection.

Judging Dolls to Reproduce

Reproducing antique dolls is an art and the most wonderful of pastimes. Reproductions should be made of the very rarest, the finest, the most expensive and the most beautiful dolls. The idea is to have a doll that you could not buy or find; one that would be too expensive for most collectors to buy. Only fine and rare dolls are worth reproducing. Other dolls such as the common open-mouth German dolls are cheap enough to buy (sometimes less than the time and money to make a reproduction). With antique dolls the value is apt to go up, but a reproduction's value may never increase while there are antique dolls like it still available.

We have recently seen another surge in the price of the rare beauties. The A.T.'s are a good example. During the summer of 1989 the prices ranged from $37,000 for a tiny A.T., to over $68,000 for a large A.T. These were auction prices. So you can see why a nice reproduction A.T. would be worthwhile to add to any doll collection. The fabulous H-Dolls are a collector's dream. Yet the price is so high, that for most, a reproduction doll will have to suffice. This is when we appreciate the people who provide the antique dolls so that molds can be made. (A reproduction is an exact copy of the antique with the exception of errors or misplaced lines, which, of course, are not copied.)

There are many ugly, cheaply made and poorly painted antique dolls on the market at reasonable prices. These are *not* what reproduction dolls

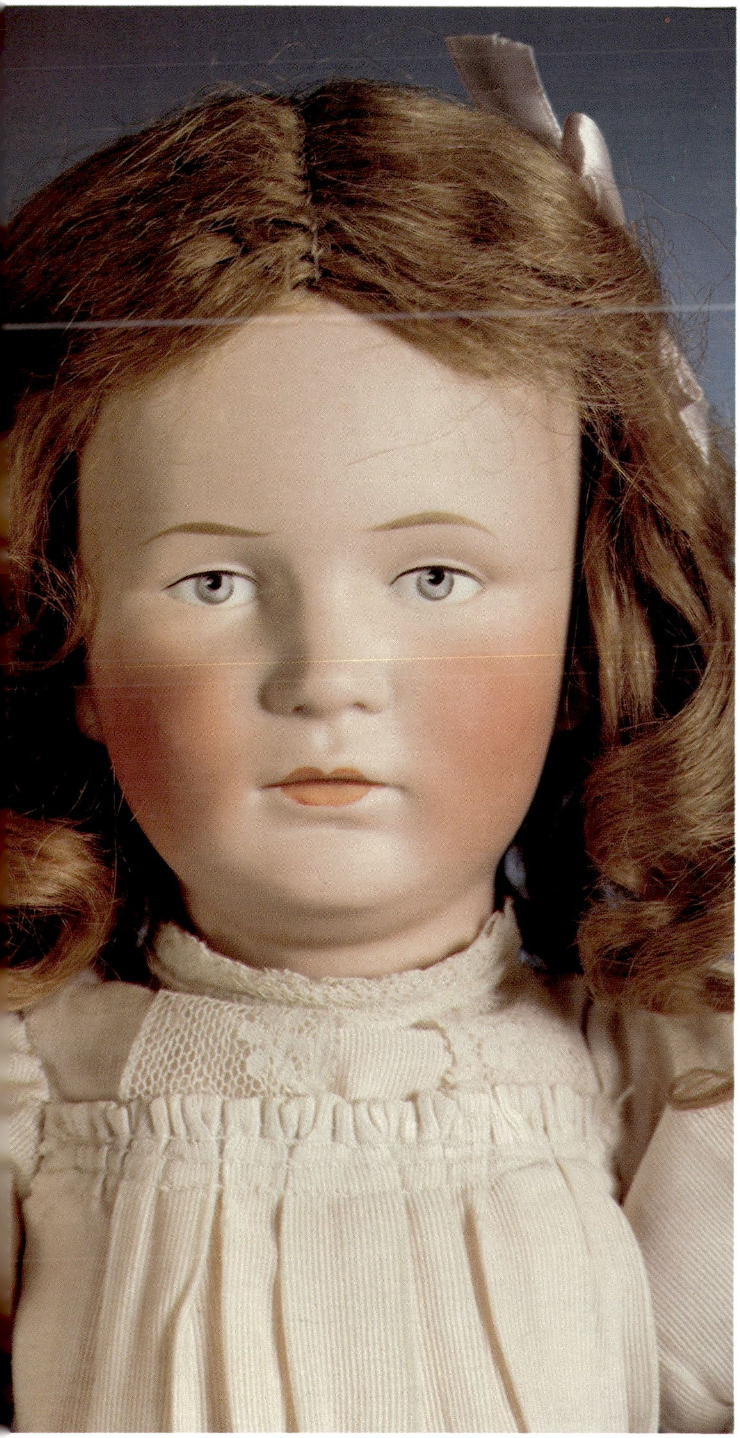

This rare character doll by Frans Schmidt would make an interesting and worthwhile mold for a reproduction.

Brus are the standing favorite for reproductions. This is Bru Jne 9. It is a challenge to get that "Bru look" in a reproduction.

MILDRED SEELEY'S EDJS EDUCATIONAL DOLL JUDGING SYSTEM

JUDGING EXERCISE

Left, four Steiners to choose from: (L-R) Doll 1 is in pink cotton and is marked A 9 Le Parisien; Doll 2 is marked Steiner F A 11 and is in an antique dress; Doll 3 is marked A 13 Parisien and she is dressed in a copy of an antique costume; Doll 4, in mauve silk, is dressed in a copy of an antique dress. She is marked FIRE B 11.

All of these dolls have excellent bisque, and the bodies are in good condition. All four bodies are different. Dolls 1 and 2 have straight legs. Doll 4 has jointed wrists. Doll 3 has bisque hands. Dolls 1 and 2 have human hair wigs; 3 and 4 have mohair wigs.

Which doll do you want for your collection? Which will surely win a blue ribbon? Which would you say had "universal appeal?"

Stop: Judge these dolls yourself.

Anyone of these four Steiners would be great in a collection. I love them all. As for the blue ribbon winners, both Dolls 3 and 4 will take blue ribbons in any doll crowd. Doll 3 has perfect bisque hands, an original wig and an exceptionally fine copy of an old costume. Doll 4 is extremely rare and has an open mouth with teeth. She also has wire eyes that work. She is well dressed.

Doll 2 has universal appeal. I know because I used her face on a doll plate, and the plate sold exceptionally well.

Left, 27" marked A.T. These make wonderful dolls to reproduce, and they should be copied exactly.

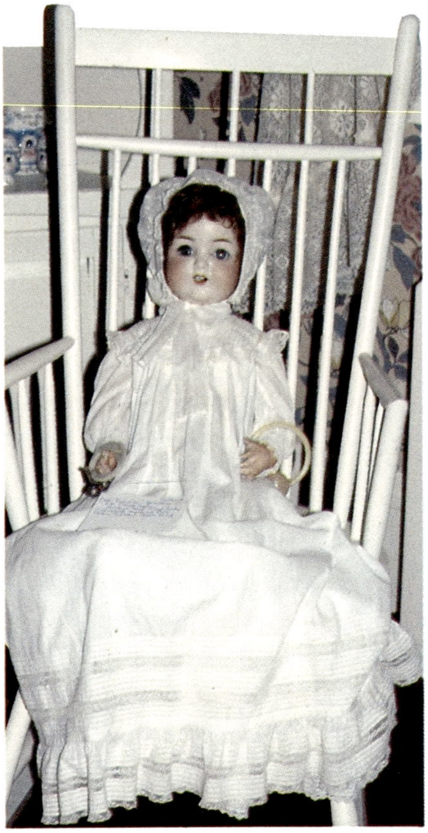

Dolls in a museum do not need to be perfect like this one.

Much of the educational value of the doll in a museum depends on the doll's labeling.

are all about. Consider the cost involved with making molds. It is foolhardy to make or buy molds for reproductions of these plentiful, open-mouth dolls. What would you have by making an exact copy of one of these? It would be wasted time, paint and talent. Put your best efforts to work making dolls that you could only dream of owning, such as Brus, Schmitts, A.T.'s, Jumeaux, H-Dolls or the other fabulous rare old French dolls. German characters are also expensive and rare, and they are worth copying too.

I feel it is a shame for our fine, talented reproduction artists (who make dolls finer than the antique) to waste their time, money and effort copying inferior dolls.

So make a judgment, and make it carefully when you choose dolls to reproduce.

Judging Dolls for a Museum

Doll museums with French, German and American dolls are scattered across America, Europe, Australia and Japan. Large and small doll museums are coming and going all the time. The small, privately owned museums have to struggle to make ends meet, and here and there, some are dissolved while others are just starting.

Judging dolls to be purchased for a museum is quite different from judging dolls for any other collection. Here you must think: Why are the dolls being placed on exhibit? Why will people come, perhaps pay, to see the dolls? Mainly doll museums serve three purposes—to educate the onlookers, to entertain, and to preserve the collection.

The selector or judge of what goes into the museum must look for the very beautiful, the unusual, the extremely rare, and the entertaining. There must be a wide selection of types, kinds, sizes and shapes. There must be something for everyone and every age. There must be dolls that will appeal and educate the doll lovers and the general public.

Usually these dolls are set up with their faces to the crowd. No one will ever take them out, strip them down to look at their bodies, or take off their wigs and pates to peer into their heads—like one would in a home collection.

Therefore while judging dolls for a museum or exhibit, the criteria is quite different from judging for investment purposes or a private collection. Rarity is extremely important in the museum collection. Rare dolls provide the bait to get the doll collectors from all over the world to come and view the collection. These dolls will make effective advertising. If the museum collected dolls such as a Marque, Mothereau, Huret, Thuillier, H's, the K*R characters, the S & H 900 series etc., collectors will go to the museum for educational reasons and to be familiar with these faces.

The doll's rarity is much more important than its condition. A cracked or broken doll can serve the museum's purposes. For example, the museum doesn't need to put on the exhibit card, "This doll has a hairline crack all the way down the back of its head." The important message is the doll's marking and history.

Bru Jne 5. In a museum it doesn't matter that the doll has a cracked wrist. Museum dolls don't have to be blue ribbon dolls.

28" Steiner Series C.

22" Andre Jean Thuillier. An appraiser must recognize exceptional dolls and photograph them as part of the appraisal.

Appraising Dolls

Appraising dolls for insurance, for resale, or for probate court are just other forms of doll judging that must be done in much the same way as previously discussed. The doll must be identified by its markings; it must be measured; its condition noted; and its value established. Usually, a photograph is necessary too.

First and foremost the appraiser must have a vast knowledge of dolls and be able to identify a majority of the dolls at a glance. If there are some dolls she doesn't know, she must locate them in books in order to establish their value. She must be able to pick out rare and valuable dolls. She must be keen enough to see even the smallest hairline crack, identify replaced parts, and know if the head and body belong together. She must be especially sharp in identifying reproduction dolls or parts that are reproductions. Reproduction dolls are all over the market today many of which are painted better and have better bodies than the antiques from which they were copied. However, reproduction prices are far below the price of an antique doll.

An appraiser must handle old dolls with care. Any rough handling or mistreatment of old costumes or bisque could depreciate the doll's value. Dolls should be handled carefully, and they should be redressed so that not even a single item gets lost or put on another doll.

Certain personal qualifications are necessary for an appraiser, such as integrity, accuracy and a general appreciation of dolls.

Income for the Appraiser

In general the price for a doll appraisal is high, but not when you consider that a lifetime of study in dolls must precede any appraisal work. Dolls are one of the most difficult objects to appraise, because there is so much to know. Unless you are knowledgeable in their construction, costuming, and history, mistakes can be made.

Doll appraisers usually get from $85 to $100 per hour. Expenses are added for typing, photography and travel costs. Some appraisers arrive at their price another way. They do small jobs (under $6,000 in appraisal value) for $100.

Most people will want an estimate of how much the appraisal will run before they decide on who or whether it will be done. Estimating the time to examine dolls and locate markings is not easy. This is where the doll expert saves the doll collector or estate appraisal expense. She knows at a glance at least 95% of the dolls and their current value. The less experienced doll appraiser, or the one with limited association with antique dolls, will have to carry books and/or research material when she needs to be certain about today's prices.

You need to know how many dolls you can do in an hour in order to give an estimate of appraisal costs. The number of dolls per hour will vary according to the dolls, the place, and the light you are given to work in.

It is most convenient and a timesaver to have a skilled assistant. If there are many dolls, you need someone to write down the numbers and

Above, rare antique dolls such as these Poulbouts, owned by Jay and Susan Foreman, could easily stump any appraiser.

This lovely little china doll with brush-stroked hair belongs to Colette Keneally. She was dressed by Jeanette Finan many, many years ago. This doll would be appraised for about $1,000, which is high for chinas. But she is absolutely perfect and perfectly costumed.

your comments about the doll while you are examining it. Sometimes the assistant redresses the dolls and helps to keep the dolls organized or in groups. Working with my husband, I can evaluate 150 dolls in 5 hours. Ordinarily, I can depend completely on my knowledge, and there will be none or only a few dolls that I will have to research either for identity or value. Afterwards, photos of the dolls worth over $2,000.00 are taken and the list is typed.

If you have reason to research certain dolls, consider this part of your education, and don't charge the patron for what you don't know. You will develop better skills as you continue to appraise. Remember, it is far better to research the dolls than to make a mistake.

There is another consideration when evaluating dolls for an estate. You must do the work at the convenience of the person holding the dolls and within the time limit set by the attorney or bank.

The type of appraisal also affects how much time an appraiser must spend on a doll. It all depends on what exactly the appraisal is for, because this may make a big difference in what is recorded and the estimated value. The person hiring the appraiser must clearly understand this before the work is begun.

For example, while appraising dolls for an estate that is going through probate court, the dolls are given what is referred to as "fair market value." This is the price an ordinary person selling the dolls to a neighbor could get for the doll. This is far less than a doll dealer who has customers all over a wide area could demand for the doll. Here, too, the person wanting the appraisal is usually the one paying the inheritance tax. He is hoping to keep the appraisal low to save money on inheritance taxes.

26" Hilda by Kestner, a blue ribbon baby. Be careful appraising Hilda, because her value has gone up in leaps and bounds.

Insurance Appraisal

Doll appraisal for insurance purposes is somewhat different and much more complete and exacting. The doll description must be accurate enough so that the doll can be recognized by its height, markings, color of hair, type of eyes, costume type and color, and anything unusual or special about that doll. The value placed on the doll is not the same as for probate. Here, the *replacement cost* of that particular doll at the present time is important. The doll's value must be updated every year or so to keep the price current. Some insurance companies want photos, others don't. Remind the collector that the dolls should be insured at replacement cost.

One way to figure the value on each doll is to use the price paid for the doll, plus an 8% increase per year. (We all know this is not accurate for certain dolls like Brus that have gone up 60% in one year, or for chinas that have not gone up at all for several years.) Overall, this method will average for most dolls.

If the dolls have been a gift, average the present-day selling price of three identical dolls or nearly alike dolls. Use auction prices for the current year.

If the doll collection has been inherited, it is quite possible that the estate has already had an appraisal of the doll collection. There is no reason why this should not be available to you. If no appraisal was made, then it is wise to have one done. You need the appraisal, not only to get the doll collection insured, but to know exactly what you have.

After you have studied and learned how to appraise dolls for all kinds of reasons, you should go to your insurance company to get your own dolls insured. You will probably be shocked when you find out the insurance company will not accept your appraisal of your own dolls. Instead, you must have an outsider come in and make the appraisal. I cannot stress enough how much care you must take in selecting an appraiser.

Doll appraisal for resale is not different from insurance purposes. Usually, the person getting the appraisal done is the owner of the doll. The owner must consider whether she is selling the collection as a whole, including the good and the bad, or if she is selling each doll individually. The price will be higher if the dolls are to be individually priced. You may be asked to come up with two prices on the collection.

Appraising Reproduction and Limited Edition Dolls

How do you appraise reproduction, limited edition or artists dolls?

This is a difficult question. It would be much easier to give an answer when after the dolls are a "collectible" age or over 35 years old. After waiting 35 years, we would be able to tell which dolls stand up to the test of time. We could tell which dolls were made by the thousands, and thousands still remain. We could know which dolls had that charm, that special appeal that makes them as loved after 35 years as when they were first purchased.

Above, two 13" Jumeaux were appraised and insured for $300 each in 1960! Now they are in my collection and the one with the closed mouth is insured for $2,000 and the open-mouthed one for $1,500. Your insurance must keep up with the times and changing prices.

27" Jumeau "Lady of the Evening." Very rare dolls like this are hard to appraise.

Whether dolls of these types will be of any value as investment dolls remains to be seen in the next 35 to 100 years. Today, dolls that were made in the thousands, such as the general run of Armand Marseille, are still not investment dolls. Most of these modern dolls are created in numbers too large to be rare or special—even in 100 years.

In regards to appraising these modern dolls for insurance purposes or resale, I am going to be a little hard on those who collect these. In general the doll can be appraised at cost, although sometimes the value has gone down. For instance, "three mint-in-box" Cabbage Patch dolls were recently sold at auction for $10.

For the most part, use the cost of the doll for the first five years, then re-evaluate. You can't appraise dolls that you have made yourself or your own reproduction. This must be done by a qualified appraiser. She will judge the finished product's current value, not the time, materials, or money you have put into the doll. This value will be somewhere around the selling price of the doll.

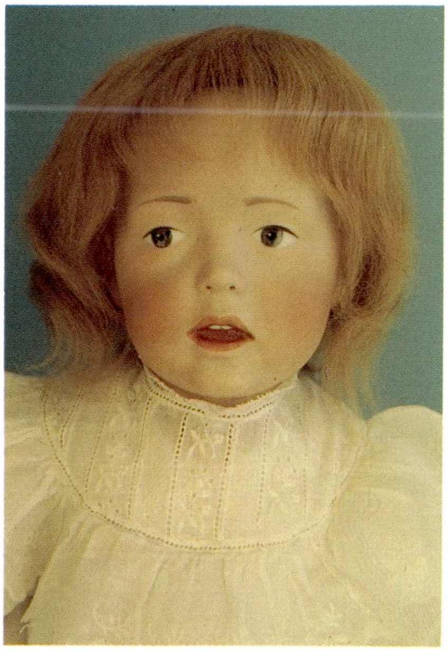

*The soft character modeling around the mouth and chin make this K*R 112 a wanted doll.*

The Appraisal

The appraisal consists of a typewritten list of the dolls in the collection. They are usually grouped in like kinds by materials, such as bisque, wood, cloth, composition, etc. Each doll is judged for its rarity, age, markings, condition and costume.

Each doll, unless they are of minimal value, is listed separately by height, maker, markings, defects, fair market value or replacement cost.

Any doll of great value, such as a Bru, should be photographed. This is to prevent a mistake in identification. The price of the photograph is added on to the appraisal costs. Some dolls of minimal value may be grouped together. An example would be 20 all-bisque Japanese dolls, 9 handmade cloth dolls, or 18 all-bisque reproductions.

There are numerous books available with pictures of dolls and their values. I especially like to use the auction catalogs that I have marked with the selling prices. Price guides should only be used as *guides*. They only give the range of values for dolls in mint condition. If you are researching a doll, always try to find more than one price for that same doll. Be sure to check the year the book you are referring to was published.

For the appraisal, photograph any doll over $2,000 in value. This 17"Pan by Henri Delcroix is valued about $9,000.

24" doll marked H. Her appealing face makes her choice.

Choosing an Antique or Collectible Doll to Exhibit

Let's say there is a doll convention coming up—perhaps it's a year away. The first step is registering for the convention. The second step is making hotel reservations, and the third is making plane reservations or travel arrangements to the show. Each of these things will have a bearing on which doll or dolls you will choose to exhibit.

Where the convention is held, the distance from your home, and the time of year, will all make a difference in your choice. If you are staying in the same hotel where the show is held, it will be easier to take the dolls into the exhibit room and pick them up. How you are going to travel to the show (by plane or car) will also have much to do with the dolls you select. Very large dolls can be carried in the car as easily as smaller ones; whereas, carrying large dolls on a plane may be hazardous to the doll and very inconvenient. Keep these things in mind before you start. Also consider the materials that are easy to pack and least likely to break.

Study the categories the convention committee sent to you. Check out all the possibilities that you have and write them down. Go back and review the history of these dolls to be sure that you have the right dates for the doll and that they fit the category. At every exhibit there are dolls sitting by the side because they are in the wrong class or do not fit the category in some way.

Usually the categories are so varied that almost any collector can find a place to exhibit one or some of her dolls.

Choose the very best you have. It should be the rarest, the most authentic, the most original (parts and costume), as well as the doll in the best condition for each exhibit category that you intend to enter.

From this group, select dolls that will fit your way of travelling. For instance, if you are going from coast to coast and you have to stop once or twice and change airplanes, carry the dolls that will be the most convenient. Soft dolls will pack in your luggage and will not add problems or worries. Most composition, paper mache, or wood dolls are safe to pack in luggage. These should be wrapped first in plastic bubble wrap and then packed in the center of the suitcase with clothing on all sides. It is best to look for delicate parts, like hands and feet, and put a little extra packing around them so they cannot be squashed. Sometimes it is easier to pack them in a box and make some kind of carrying handle on top of the box. The box will go with your luggage and will take quite a beating during travel, so do not take chances with anything really breakable.

I have carried many bisque dolls home on airlines. From the UFDC convention in San Antonio, I brought home five French Fashions in perfect condition. I prewrapped the bisque hands. Then I rolled the whole doll in fine bubble plastic. I held the wrap with rubber bands. I tied all five dolls in a bundle and put one more layer of bubble plastic around them. I placed the bundle into a shopping bag which more or less fit under the seat ahead of me.

Many times I have carried two or three medium-size bisque dolls in the same manner. I have also carried one large bisque doll wrapped in

This little 15" Simon and Halbig (no number) is so skinny, she could be rolled up in bubble wrap and carried in a pocketbook. Her hair and clothing are all original. Her little boy is numbered 142 with nothing else.

Käthe Kruse dolls. These types of dolls will travel safely and are blue ribbon worthy.

31" Bruno Schmidt doll marked BSW in heart.

bubble plastic and placed in a box about the length of the doll. This large doll traveled in the compartment above the seats. Smaller dolls could be wrapped and put around the large doll in the same box.

However you carry your doll, you are taking some chances on her being broken, stolen, or damaged. Although the doll is probably covered in a home owner's fine arts policy, most dolls cannot be replaced with money. But do not let this scare you out of the joy of sharing dolls.

This transportation problem can sometimes eliminate your very best doll and your very best chance for a blue ribbon. Because the conventions are in different places each year, perhaps next year it will be in driving distance. Plan your exhibit two or three years ahead of time.

But there is another way. If you don't try to take all ten of the dolls that are allowed, you could lap-carry your one special doll. Wrap her in plastic bubble wrap even while carrying her, because this prevents the person sitting next to you from playing with her.

19" Mothereau marked B M. She is a good doll to exhibit, her blue ribbon hangs on her back.

24" and 16" Figure A Steiners. Both dolls are excellent examples of Steiners.

This 28" EJA could go to a convention if you are driving or in a well-wrapped box if you are flying. While flying, you can store her in the overhead luggage compartment. She probably won't get a blue ribbon, because she has a homemade mohair wig, not her original wig.

19" E J Jumeau is the perfect blue ribbon doll in mint condition.

MILDRED SEELEY'S EDJS EDUCATIONAL DOLL JUDGING SYSTEM

JUDGING EXERCISE

Five little German Googlies: (L-R) 241, JDK 221, Einco 8123, Heubach Koppelsdorf 318 and AM 323.

Googlies are a fun doll. They are cheerful little things to have about your house. Which one of these would you want in your collection? Which is the rarest or the most common? Are any of these blue ribbon dolls?

Stop: Judge these dolls yourself.

After examining the condition of all five dolls, it is clear that none are really "mint-mint." All five have been played with. Dolls 2 and 3 have their original clothing. Doll 3's clothing is in the best condition. Dolls 2, 3 and 5 have their original wigs.

Personally, I like the impish grin on Doll 1 for my collection. Dolls 3 and 4 are both rare Googlies. I have never seen either of these at auction. Doll 5 is the most common; she is often found.

Googlies originally had their eyes set so that they would sleep. All of these dolls sleep with the exception of Doll 5. I would give Dolls 2 and 3 blue ribbons. Dolls 1 and 4 have been redressed and their wigs replaced so I would give them red ribbons. I would give Doll 5 a white ribbon because: she is redressed; her eyes do not work; her shoes and socks are new; and one finger is repaired. If I were pinning on rosettes, I would put it on the Einco (Doll 3). His eyes are connected to a lever on the back of his head which moves the eyes from side-to-side or to close them.

31" F.G. by Gaultier is a good buy at auction.

Buying Dolls at Auction

The first step in deciding to buy at auctions is purchasing the auction catalog. If you are not on the auction house's list, then you must watch auction ads in the doll magazines. Auction catalogs are usually available at least two weeks before the auction. The catalogs are now expensive. They run anywhere from $15.00 to $32.00. This usually includes the prices realized that are mailed after the auction. These catalogs are like any other fine catalog, they are the "salesman" for the auction house. Many of these catalogs are works of art put together with fine color photographs on the finest glossy paper. The dolls are arranged to present each doll at its very best. (Watch out or the photo alone will get you.) It is the auction's aim to get the very highest prices possible for each and every doll.

These dated catalogs with the prices realized for each doll are fine reference books for any doll collector. Many of these photographs will also serve as references for doll artists to paint from. Judges can use them for comparing reproductions to antiques, too. The money spent on auction catalogs is not wasted, even if you don't go to the auction or buy anything.

Step two is to study the whole auction catalog for dolls that are interesting. Use all of your reference books to further check into the dolls you are interested in buying. This practice is good for increasing your knowledge, even if you don't buy a doll. Read the catalog description carefully. If there is nothing that indicates that the clothing is original or describes what the condition of the clothing is in, then assume the costume is not original. If the doll is listed as "generally excellent" that does not mean that the doll is perfect. If the whole doll is not pictured, perhaps the costume leaves something to be desired, or the proportion of the doll is not correct or something else is wrong. If the doll has marked shoes, costume or body, the auction people *will* say so. Any good points on dolls are always mentioned. If a photo is taken from the side, you better check the eyes carefully before buying.

Step three is to select a doll that you wish to purchase along with two or three alternatives. I have often decided on a doll from the catalog; but after I arrive at the viewing, I discover that the doll turns me off or that there is something wrong with her.

Mark down the top price you will bid for each doll you are interested in. Do this in code to prevent someone from looking over your shoulder and knowing your top bid.

Step four is to go to the auction viewing room as early as possible. Establish your credit with the desk and get your bidding number. Go directly to the dolls you selected from the catalog. Ask one of the assistants to aid you while looking carefully into the head and examining the doll. Judge the doll more or less as you would an antique at a doll show. You cannot undress the dolls in the auction viewing room, but you can look under the clothing and also ask to see the markings. Look carefully for cracks because these are sometimes missed in the listings. Note if you like her and adjust your top bidding price to *how much* you like her.

Portrait Jumeau marked only 9. The older the Jumeau, the higher the price.

This 24" Steiner Figure A was a nice buy at auction. The dress, by Suzanne Pirtle, was copied exactly from another Steiner at auction.

Now go over the other dolls that you had considered as alternates. Check each carefully and adjust your top bid on each then cover all the other dolls exhibited if you have time.

At the auction, dolls come up for sale in the order they are listed in the catalog. This often makes a problem for the bidder to get just the doll she wants.

For example, if the bidder has a list of dolls that she wants to bid on, and her last choice comes up first, should she bid on it? If she does, what if she is the top bidder on that doll, buys it, and then doesn't have enough money to bid on the doll she really wants?

My strategy is to wait until the doll I want the most comes up for bid, and I select my alternate choices from those dolls that come up after the doll I really want.

Of course this just can't always work. Sometimes the bidding will start above what I intended to pay, and I'm out before I start. Tell yourself there will be another auction.

Step five is to pay for the doll you were the highest bidder on. Then pick up the doll (you can do this anytime during the auction or after it is over). The girls wrapping the dolls like to hurry you, but don't let them. Look over your purchase carefully. If there is anything seriously wrong that was not listed in the catalog, do not accept the doll. If the shoes or hat are missing, get them now or you will never get them.

Auction buying is a little scary. It is a gamble. Still the best prices and values come through the auction houses.

The collector must be sharp to detect defects; patient to get the doll she wants; and confident to maintain complete control over her bidding.

Doll auctions are fun and educational for any doll collector, judge, costumer, or reproduction artist. You can see and study firsthand what has taken someone a lifetime to collect. You can also study the costumes, take notes and make drawings. You can practice doll judging and give them imaginary ribbons. Some will already have ribbons and you can rejudge these to see if you agree. If you are a collector, you can study the old dolls to see which ones you will eventually want to add to your collection. You can judge all the dolls as a collection and decide whether you think it was a good collection or a poor one and why.

Auctions are one of the best study places for all doll people. And you meet the wonderful other doll collectors from all over. You can see I just love doll auctions. Many of my finest dolls have come from auctions. I have also made many doll friends at auctions.

Wax peddler doll with cloth body and leather hands. Her boots were made on her feet. In a class with peddlers, she would rate a blue ribbon because she has been left untouched for at least forty years—perhaps ever since she was made.

Unmarked French Fashion is 27". She is wearing her blue ribbon from 1968.

MILDRED SEELEY'S EDJS EDUCATIONAL DOLL JUDGING SYSTEM

JUDGING EXERCISE

Four German character dolls all made between 1910 and 1915. From the photo, try to decide which ribbons these dolls should receive. Also try to select one to buy for resale, and another one to keep in your own collection.

*(L-R) Doll 1 is a S&H 151; Doll 2 is a Frans Schmidt 1263; Doll 3 is a K*R 112; Doll 4 is a Kestner 180.*

The condition of the dolls after a close inspection is as follows: Doll 1 is in mint condition; Doll 2 is completely original, but her dress has many tiny beetle holes; Doll 3 has been redressed, has terrible new shoes, and a tiny hairline crack on its forehead; Doll 4 is in excellent condition, but it may have been re-dressed in old material.

Stop: Judge these dolls yourself.

All four dolls are precious collector's favorites. I put blue ribbons on Dolls 1 and 2 because they are the most perfect characters I've ever found in these rare dolls. I gave Doll 4 a red ribbon, but I could have given him a blue one too. I gave Doll 3 a white ribbon, because of his hairline crack and poor shoes.

*As for the one to resell, the K*R 112 (Doll 3) is the highest priced and the rarest doll. His value might go up faster than any of the other dolls—in spite of his hairline crack.*

As for my own collection, if I could have just one, I would choose the darling little boy 180 Kestner (Doll 4). I could look at him every day and never get tired of him.

My selections may not agree with yours, but each collector should make up her own mind for her own reasons.

If you are selecting a doll by telephone or from an auction catalog for an absentee bid, you will have to decide on the doll from a picture just like this. Practice opens our eyes and makes us better collectors.

Conclusion

Judging dolls for our own collection or for doll shows is not something that can be covered in a few pages or even a single book. It would take volumes to cover the subject completely. In this book we have only tried to steer the many people involved in judging dolls in the right direction. There are many dolls and classifications for dolls that I have not even touched upon due to the large variety of dolls in the world.

Many people have written to me with suggestions and help for this book. The many doll judges that came to my home for two- or three-day seminars all contributed their ideas. Hundreds of dollmakers sent pictures of their wonderful blue ribbon dolls—I wish we could have included them all. Judges from across America, Australia and New Zealand have sent their judging sheets for comparison.

I do want doll collectors and show judges to take this work seriously—to do what they can to improve the exhibits and collections. Most of all, I want to keep the whole doll world filled with happiness and with happy people having a wonderful time with dolls, like I do.

I believe it was Alexander Girard who said something like, "Toys represent a microcosm of man's world and dreams. They exhibit fantasy, imaginations, humor and love. They are an individual record and expression of man's indigenous unsophisticated imagination."

Right, 24" rare Jumeau Character marked 211. "You came dreaming of a blue ribbon and of new glory unfolding. You put forth every effort but the cordon bleu was not for you. So cry if it will help."

BABY MINE

About the Author

Mildred & Vernon Seeley

Mildred Seeley is well known in the doll world. She is a dollmaker and collector and has been involved with dolls all her life.

Judging Dolls is Mildred's 19th book in the last 20 years by various publishers.

An active member of the United Federation of Doll Clubs, she has worked hard to get people all over the world interested in collecting dolls. In that pursuit, Mildred founded the Doll Artisan Guild, an organization for dollmakers.

Mildred is affectionately called the "First Lady of Dolls," a title bestowed on her by the International Ceramic Association and Expo Enterprises. She was given this recognition in 1982 at the California Doll Convention.

Always interested in telling the public about dolls, Mildred founded and edited *The Dollmaker* magazine for a number of years. She was also the founder and special editor of the *Doll Artisan* magazine, published by the Doll Artisan Guild.

Mildred's appreciation of dolls is heightened by her appreciation of art. She holds a Bachelor's degree in art, and a Master's in art education.